Behold

Your

Mother

Priests Speak

about Mary

A heartfelt and joyful odyssey of faith.

From the foreword by Most Reverend Donald W. Wuerl
Archbishop of Washington, D.C.

. . . an invitation to give thanks for [one's] priestly vocation.

Most Reverend Wilton D. Gregory
Archbishop of Atlanta

This gem of a book invites all the Catholic faithful, but especially priests, to find Jesus more personally through a renewed love of his mother.

J. Augustine Di Noia, O.P.

If a priest is puzzled by pain, evil, temptation, and other burdens, then this book indicates how he can identify with Mary's sorrows, her questionings, and her acceptance.

Most Reverend Tom M. Burns
Marist, Priest, and Bishop (UK Armed Forces)

This book will invigorate those for whom Our Lady is already a part of their spirituality; it could also resurrect a place for Mary in the prayer of those priests who, for whatever reason, have over the years seemingly forgotten her.

Father Joseph M. Champlin
Diocese of Syracuse, N.Y.

Behold Your Mother

Priests Speak

about Mary

Edited by Stephen J. Rossetti

ave maria press AmP notre dame, indiana

Nihil Obstat: Rev. Msgr. Michael P. Minehan, J.C.L.

Imprimatur: Most Rev. James M. Moynihan
           Bishop of Syracuse
           Given at Syracuse, New York, on February 2, 2007

Founded in 1865, Ave Maria Press is a ministry of the Indiana Province of Holy Cross.

www.avemariapress.com

ISBN-10 1-59471-028-7   ISBN-13 978-1-59471-028-5

Cover and text design by John Carson.

Cover photo © Erich Lessing / Art Resource, NY

Printed and bound in the United States of America.

Library of Congress Cataloging-in-Publication Data
Behold your Mother : priests speak about Mary / edited by Stephen J. Rossetti ; foreword by Donald W. Wuerl.
    p. cm.
  Includes bibliographical references.
  ISBN-13: 978-1-59471-028-5 (pbk.)
  ISBN-10: 1-59471-028-7 (pbk.)
  1. Mary, Blessed Virgin, Saint. 2. Catholic Church--Doctrines. I. Rossetti, Stephen J., 1951-

  BT603.B44 2007
  232.91--dc22

                                    2007013299

To all the mothers of our priests:

Thank you for saying yes to our lives.

Contents

Foreword

Most Reverend Donald W. Wuerl, S.T.D.
Archbishop of Washington

Devotion to Mary has always been a hallmark of priestly spirituality. For centuries, priests have found in the Mother of Jesus a great source of personal support and a ready intercessor with her Son. In reading these reflections on Mary seen through the eyes of priests, one senses immediately a confirmation of the long-standing recognition that priests love and pray to the Blessed Mother. Monsignor Stephen Rossetti's collection of well-written and inspirational glimpses into the many-faceted relationship that Mary has with her Son and, therefore with his priests, offers enriching insight into a great priestly tradition.

Perhaps because Mary is the model of what our faith should be, we priests, who strive to live as fully as we can a life of faith, and encourage others to do the same, find devotion to her comes easily. Mary was a human being who had to struggle to hear and accept God's word and to grasp the mysterious ways in which God works. She did so with such consummate fidelity that she is forever the example of what we mean by faith—true, profound faith.

Reading the Marian vignettes in this remarkable book, we are fully aware that we cannot equal Mary in the wondrous mysteries in which she participated and in the privileges she received. But we can certainly emulate her faith. Mary said, in effect, "Although I do not always understand the unfolding of God's plan and God's providential order, nonetheless, if God calls, I accept. If God challenges, I respond."

A priest, whose life is defined by his call and most particularly his response to the call, can so comfortably identify with Mary. The faith of every priest, the faith of every believer, is challenged to be the faith of Mary. The meaning of Mary's role in God's plan of salvation is summed up in Paul's letter to the Galatians: "But when the fullness of time had come, God sent his Son, born of a woman, born under the law, to ransom those under the law, so that we might receive adoption" (Gal 4:4). We, as priests, are the heralds of that message and the ministers of the mysteries that unite women and men with Christ so that they might receive adoption.

It is both the greatness of the mission and the fragility of our own involvement in that sacred action that bring us so often to our knees in prayer with our hearts turned to the Mother of God, the Mother of Jesus, the Mother of the Church. Reading these stories of personal faith, experience, and devotion, I was reminded of the significant role Mary has always played in my life and ministry. In the parish where I grew up, the principal image of Mary was that of Our Lady of Perpetual Help. One of the places I first celebrated Mass as a newly ordained priest in Rome included the Shrine of Our Lady of Perpetual Help. To this day, I carry in my wallet a small, plastic version of that same representation of Mary. Today in my new responsibilities at the Basilica of the National Shrine of the Immaculate Conception, I am all the more strengthened with the realization that I can stop at the chapel of Our Lady of Perpetual Help every time I visit that extraordinary national house of Mary.

Many priests I know speak freely of their great devotion to the Mother of God. A few have even written reflections on her. But none have done so in such a wide-ranging and truly touching manner as those priests, whose thoughts and experiences concerning Mary are gathered in this heartfelt and joyful odyssey of faith put together by Monsignor Rossetti.

Behold Your Mother is one more sign of what I believe is a great renewal in the life of the Church today. Just as there is a resurgence of spirituality and a hunger for good, solid, faith-filled catechesis, so there is also a rekindling of love, priestly love, focused on Jesus' Mother and our Mother. In his introduction, Msgr. Rossetti poses the question, "Have we priests forgotten our Mother?" It does not take long into this collection of spiritual memoirs to be able to respond emphatically and happily, "No!" It is good to be reminded of just how wonderful is our long-standing and holy relationship in prayer and devotion to the Mother of God.

October 2, 2006

Introduction

Rev. Msgr. Stephen J. Rossetti

A few days before Christmas, I received a note from the Editorial Director of Ave Maria Press, Bob Hamma. Bob relayed an experience he had. He was in New York and standing in line for communion at St. Patrick's Cathedral on the Feast of the Immaculate Conception, and an inspiration came to him: he should publish a book on the role of Mary in the spiritual lives of priests. He then wrote to me, "I haven't seen much lately on this subject, and since it is a very traditional idea, it would seem that the renewal of priestly spirituality in these times could benefit from the focus on this dimension of priestly spirituality." He confided, "I guess that's about as close as Mary can come to hitting me over the head, so I thought I should get started on exploring it." Bob is not one usually given to spiritual enthusiasms and inspirations, so I knew this was a special grace.

Like Bob, I have not heard much about the subject in recent years. I have been at scores of priest convocations and other priestly gatherings, and the subject of a Marian spirituality for priests seems all but forgotten. The old days when priests would finger their rosary beads while driving their cars to pastoral stops have largely disappeared. I seldom hear priests preaching about Our Lady. In many parishes, Marian devotions and statues have disappeared or been relegated to a forgotten corner of the parish's life. Have we priests forgotten our Mother?

Post-Vatican II Refocusing

It is understandable that we have ended up in this place. In pre-Vatican II days, many priests experienced excesses of Marian piety. One priest complained to me that he saw people walking right by the Blessed Sacrament in his church without the slightest acknowledgment and then proceeding directly to the statue of Mary and praying. Similarly, another priest told me that when he mentioned to some of the laity that Jesus alone is Lord and Savior and that Mary must be considered in a subordinate role to Jesus, they looked surprised. Excesses in Marian piety were apparently contaminating people's theology. As theologian Hans Urs Von Balthasar noted:

> . . . they thus elevate Mary into the divine sphere and so overlook Christ's decisive work . . . the above-mentioned impression can be accurate in the case of peoples who are less well catechized. . . . Marian piety, if it means to be Catholic, must not isolate itself; it must always be embedded in, and ordered to, Christ (and thus to the Trinity) and the Church.[1]

The Second Vatican Council cautioned against excesses in Marian piety. In *Lumen Gentium*, the Council Fathers wrote,

But this Synod earnestly exhorts theologians and preachers of the divine word that . . . they carefully and equally avoid the falsity of exaggeration on the one hand, and the excess of narrow-mindedness on the other. . . . Let them rightly explain the offices and privileges of the Blessed Virgin which are always related to Christ . . . (LG 67).[2]

But a full-scale looting of our Marian spirituality was not intended by the Vatican Council. While the Council did "not hesitate to profess this subordinate role of Mary" (LG 62), it also said,

This most Holy Synod . . . admonishes all the sons of the Church that the cult, especially the liturgical cult, of the Blessed Virgin, be generously fostered . . . and the practices and exercises of devotion, recommended by the magisterium of the Church toward her in the course of centuries be made of great moment (LG 67).

It is difficult for frail human beings to achieve proper balance. It appears that we move from one extreme to the next, finding the middle point of balance only in passing.

In the wake of this "re-focusing" on Jesus and apparent loss of Marian spirituality, are we doing better theologically and spiritually? We priests can confidently say that the notion of refocusing on Jesus alone as Lord and Savior is important. But I wonder if this has actually happened. When the Congregation for the Doctrine of the Faith published *Dominus Jesus*, many people within our Catholic communion took offense. While some criticized the tone of certain passages, there were others who actually criticized the essential notion that Jesus alone is Lord and Savior. They said it was harmful to our outreach to other religions. In a recent convocation of priests, I reiterated this integral Christian belief of Jesus' unique role as Savior and, surprising to me, one of the priests openly objected. Similarly, recent polls of Catholics have shown a surprising lack of belief in what the Church teaches about the real presence of Jesus in the Eucharist. Is it possible that the post-Vatican II weakening of Marian spirituality, in an attempt to refocus on Jesus, has actually had the deleterious effect of weakening our understanding of Jesus?

As we step back and view it from a distance, this should not be a surprise to us. It is Mary's role to bring us to her Son. When we distance ourselves from her, we lose an important conduit to Jesus.

Is a Marian Spirituality Optional?

In this modern era, I think many priests, including myself, viewed a Marian spirituality as something optional. We may have kept our own Marian devotion quietly alive, but we presumed it was largely a private affair, like having a devotion to a particular patron saint. Upon research and after listening to knowledgeable scholars, including the authors in this book, I have come to realize that I was mistaken.

A Marian spirituality is not an optional, private devotion. Rather, *God wills this woman to be an integral part of our Christian spiritual lives.*

As Hans Urs Von Balthasar wrote, "Whoever intends to listen to, and to heed, the gospel . . . see[s] the total picture of Mary, of her person and function, light up. Anyone who fails to do so . . . can hardly be called an attentive hearer of the Word."[3] Thus, an honest reading of the scriptures highlights the essential role of Mary.

Similarly, Cardinal Ratzinger, now Benedict XVI, wrote, "The Church neglects one of the duties enjoined upon her when she does not praise Mary. She deviates from the word of the Bible when her Marian devotion falls silent. When this happens, in fact, the Church no longer even glorifies God as she ought."[4]

These are strong words. I am convinced they are true.

Are We Better Off?

We might also ask ourselves, are priests better off focusing solely on Jesus and leaving out a private and public devotion to Mary? In my years of working with priests, my heart goes out to them. Their hours are long; they listen to many complaints; the material rewards are slight; and the road ahead can look very long and, at times, barren. I sometimes wonder what motivates these men. How do they get up, day after day, with no real thought of any earthly reward, and accomplish their ministries with such motivation and heartfelt care? These are dedicated men.

I think each of them needs some tenderness in their lives. I want each of them to have some appropriate maternal consolation and some chaste feminine warmth. This is not only possible within the context of a faithful, priestly celibacy, it positively contributes to living our lives with full integrity.

We can find some feminine connection with the women who cross our daily paths, including family members and friends. But with Mary, there is also a real feminine intimacy offered directly to priests and a path to a kind of divine feminine intimacy as well. These thoughts are echoed in Pope Benedict's writings: "We cannot praise [God] rightly if we leave her out of account. In doing so we forget something about him that must not be forgotten. What exactly? Our first attempt at an answer could be his maternal side, which reveals itself more purely and more directly in the Son's Mother than anywhere else."[5] When we lose Mary, the feminine side of God is less visible and perhaps less accessible to us.

A faithful, priestly life without Mary is possible, but it is more difficult and it is more barren. And it is not in full conformity with God's design spoken to us through the Word.

———

As you read the individual chapters by these nine exemplary priests, I recommend you not only pay attention to their theological reflections and pastoral insights but, most importantly, listen with your heart to the fervor of their spirits. What is apparent to me is that a Marian spirituality among priests is not dead. In fact, each of these men of God has kept alive and nurtured a strong personal devotion to Our Lady. Perhaps this is one of the reasons why they are, indeed, exemplary priests. The Mother of Jesus is an important pillar of their priesthoods.

In his original motivation for commissioning this work, editor Bob Hamma spoke of the need for a renewal of priestly spirituality. There are many possible ways to begin such a renewal and many possible avenues to take, but one sure way of rekindling an ardent and faithful priestly spiritual life is to begin with Mary. As we enter a time of spiritual renewal, we priests might begin by raising our eyes to the Mother of God. As John Paul II told us in *Redemptoris Mater*, "Mary does not cease to be the 'Star of the Sea' for all those who are still on the journey of faith."[6]

one

At the School of the Mother: The Marian Spirituality of John Paul II

Rev. Anthony J. Figueiredo

"**A**fter God, I owe all to my mother. She was so good! Virtue passes readily from the heart of a mother into that of her children."[1] As a seminarian and now as a priest, I have often pondered these words, spoken by the Curé of Ars, model and patron saint of parish priests. My mother bore me in the womb and defended my life from the first moment of conception. That was especially significant for me. It was the mid-1960s, a time when the drug thalidomide was being prescribed to help mothers sleep during pregnancy. Thalidomide left many newborns with shortened limbs. My mother's doctors, knowing that I was to be born with some disability, counseled both my mother and my father to have an abortion. "How is it possible to raise a child whom you know will be handicapped? The burden, the time, the suffering. . . ." On the day of my ordination to the priesthood, my parents recounted that event to me for the first time and the answer they gave the doctors: "If God has willed this child, then surely he has a marvelous plan!"

Long before I was taught the *Catechism*, my mother taught me my first prayers. Even without words, she trained me as I watched her receive Jesus in the holy Eucharist and return from the altar rails with reverence and gratitude. Each evening, my three siblings and I would kneel with her and my father around their bed to pray the rosary. How true are the words of Father Patrick Peyton: "The family that prays together, stays together." As a child growing up, I knew that the way to my father's heart was through my mother, for he would refuse her nothing. Then, much later in life and for many years, she insisted on caring at home for my bedridden father after acute diabetes, septicemia, a stroke and Parkinson's disease had robbed him of all his strength. Watching my mother, I understood the meaning of the vows spoken in the marriage between a man and a woman: " ... for better for worse, for richer for poorer, in sickness and in health. . . ."

Karol Jozef Wojtyla was just one month short of his ninth birthday when he lost his mother, Emilia Kaczorowska. She was forty-five when kidney and heart problems led to her death in 1929. Later in life, he admits that his mother's contribution to his vocation "must have been great."[2] "Over this your white grave," he wrote poetically in the spring of 1939 at the age of nineteen when visiting his mother's tomb in Kraków, "the flowers of life in white. So many years without you, how many have passed out of sight? Over this your white grave, covered for years, there is a stir in the air, something uplifting and, like death, beyond comprehension. Over this your white grave, oh, mother, can such loving cease? For all his filial adoration a prayer: Give her eternal peace."[3]

Karol turned to Mary to be his mother. From the shaping of Marian devotion in his early childhood to his final hours, when an image of the suffering Christ and a painting of the Blessed Mother hung near his bed in the papal apartment, and even in death, when a cross and the solitary letter "M" adorned his casket, the Blessed Mother never left him. At the age of thirty, the young Father Wojtyla wrote of Mary accompanying him in his final agony in a poem that was to become remarkably prophetic: "How attentive your stillness: it will always be part of me. I lift myself towards it, will one day grow so used to it that I will lay still, transparent as water vanishing into a dry riverbed, though my body will remain. Your disciples will come, and hear that my heartbeat has stopped."[4]

This maternal relationship was at the heart of Wojtyla's priestly vocation. Years later, as Pope, he would write, "On Calvary, Jesus entrusted a new motherhood to Mary when he said to her: 'Woman, behold, your son' (Jn 19:26). We cannot overlook the fact that when this motherhood was proclaimed, it was in regard to a 'priest,' the beloved disciple." According to the synoptic Gospels, the very night before Calvary, John received from Christ at the Last Supper the priesthood through the power to renew the sacrifice of the cross in the Eucharist: "Do this in memory of me" (Lk 22:19). With the other apostles, John belonged to the first group of priests; now, at Mary's side at the foot of the cross, he replaced the one supreme priest who was leaving the world. "Jesus' gaze," the Pope writes, "extended beyond John to the long series of his priests in every age until the end of the world. As he did for the beloved disciple, he made that entrustment to Mary's motherhood for them in particular, taken one by one."[5]

At the same time, Jesus also said to John: "Behold, your mother" (Jn 19:27). To the beloved disciple and priest-apostle, he entrusted the task of caring for Mary as his own mother, of loving her, venerating her, and protecting her. "These words," the Pope writes, "are the origin of Marian devotion; the fact that they were addressed to a priest is significant. Can we not then draw the conclusion that the priest is charged with promoting and developing this devotion and that he is the one primarily responsible for it?"[6]

"From that hour, the disciple took her into his own home" (Jn 19:27). Like the apostle John on Golgotha, Pope John Paul II invites priests to take Mary "to our own home" or, even better translated, "into our own affairs," by allowing her to dwell "within the home of our sacramental priesthood." Our task, following the example of the Mother of God, is to generate and regenerate fallen man to share again the life of God. In this *spiritual motherhood*, lived for priests in a manly way as a *spiritual fatherhood*, Mary mothers us into mothering.[7]

Karol Wojtyla took Mary into everything about his life, and her indwelling wove what he calls the "Marian Thread"[8] in his priestly vocation. There are at least four factors that formed that thread: (1) the Polish Marian shrines, (2) Vatican II, (3) personal suffering, and, above all, (4) the influence of Saint Louis Marie de Montfort. In each, we, too, as seminarians and priests can learn from Pope John Paul II how to take Mary as a Mother "into our own affairs."

The Polish Marian Shrines

From a young age, Karol Wojtyla worshipped at altars and shrines dedicated to the Blessed Mother. In his parish church of St. Mary at Wadowice, he recalled the chapel dedicated to Our Lady of Perpetual Help. He and other students would stop there before and after class to seek her intercession. On a hilltop in Wadowice, large numbers of the townsfolk would visit the Carmelite monastery. It was there, at the age of ten, that Karol received the scapular of Our Lady of Mount Carmel, which he wore into death. Even as a child, and still more as a priest and bishop, he would make frequent Marian pilgrimages to Kalwaria Zebrzydowska, the principal Marian shrine of the Archdiocese of Kraków, with its icon of Our Lady of the Angels. He would go there often, presenting to the Lord in prayer the struggles of the Church, especially against communism.

Czestochowa, too, the greatest Marian shrine in Poland, became a focal point in Wojtyla's life. In the fourteenth century, Prince Wladyslaw brought to the mountain of Jasna Góra a Byzantine icon of Virgin and Child, reputed to have been painted by Saint Luke on a table belonging to the Holy Family, and he put it in the care of the monastery founded there by him. It was through the "Black Madonna's" maternal intercession, the Poles claim, that God gave them victory in a series of battles. Our Lady of Czestochowa, venerated for centuries as the Queen of Poland, thus came to represent Mary's special care for the Polish people, and especially protection against their enemies.

When Karol's mother died, his grieving father, the elder Karol Wojtyla, took him to the shrine. As a young actor, his partner, Halina Królikiewicz, fell in love with him, but a mutual friend told her that Karol was already wedded to the Madonna at Czestochowa. As Archbishop of Kraków, he preached there often, seldom missing the great annual celebration of the Queenship of Mary. As Pope, he continued to pray the "Call of Jasna Góra," an evening prayer recited throughout Poland since 1954: "Mary, Mother of Poland, we are with you and we are mindful of your presence. Together with you, we keep vigil."

Scholastic theologians speak of the agility of the risen glorified body. By this, they imply that the body of a saint can move wherever the soul pleases. The dogma of the Assumption proclaims that Mary's body is risen in heaven. In her glorified flesh then, she enjoys a homely intimacy with her children in their mortal flesh. As a priest, I have made it my duty to make a pilgrimage, even of just one day, to a Marian shrine every year since my ordination. I have personally witnessed the maternal presence of Mary in places such as Jasna Góra, Lourdes, Fatima, Guadalupe, and Washington, D.C. "In all these places," Pope John Paul II testifies, "that unique testament of the crucified Lord is wonderfully actualized. In them man feels that he is entrusted and confided to Mary. He goes there in order to be with her, as with his Mother. He opens his heart to her and speaks to her about everything."[9]

Vatican II

In his first speech as Bishop of Rome on October 17, 1978, Pope John Paul II insisted that the primary duty of his pontificate would be to implement the norms and directives of the Second Vatican Council. He himself was a bishop at the Council and he made several important interventions regarding Mary. In particular, he desired that Mary be presented at the Council in her maternal relationship to the Church. Mary had built up Christ's physical body as Mother, so she continues that role in the Mystical Body. Even though the section on Mary appears at the end of the Dogmatic Constitution on the Church and not earlier as the then Archbishop Wojtyla had desired, his thought was explicitly supported by Pope Paul VI in his proclamation of Mary as "Mother of the Church" at the close of the Council's third session.

In his own pontificate, Pope John Paul II was able to elucidate his thought in two encyclicals written to coincide with the Marian Year from Pentecost 1987 to the Assumption 1988: *Redemptoris Mater* of March 25, 1987, and *Mulieris Dignitatem* of August 15, 1988, and in a series of seventy Wednesday-audience catecheses delivered between September 6, 1995, and November 12, 1997. In fidelity to the teaching of Vatican II, "motherhood" forms the underlying theme in the Pope's Mariology. From her *fiat* at the Annunciation, to her cooperation at the foot of the cross in the redemption wrought by Christ, through to her prayerful presence with the apostles awaiting the Holy Spirit at Pentecost, Mary unceasingly intercedes and cooperates as a mother in the spiritual birth and development of the sons and daughters of the Church (RM 44).

As priests, our closest relationship to a woman must be with this Mother, such that Mary becomes the mistress of our souls. "She is the longest relationship I have ever had," writes Saint John Vianney, and "she is much better still than the best of mothers."[10] As at the wedding of Cana, seeing that "they have no wine" (Jn 2:3), the Mother of Jesus stands between her Son and us. The same intercession and maternal mediation continue in heaven. She obtains for us every grace we need. Often in the course of the day—at Mass, in the rosary, in the Angelus, or at other moments—we need to pray: "Holy Mary, Mother of God, pray for us . . . *now*. . . ." This "now" represents the particular grace we need at the present moment—for example, for chastity, for obedience, for zeal in our ministry. Blessed Teresa of Calcutta once told me that this is why I needed to pray to the Mother of Jesus. Does the Son ever refuse the request of his Mother?

Personal Suffering

Pope John Paul II's life was marked by suffering. Even before he was born, his infant sister, Olga, died, bringing great grief to his parents and brother. Just three years after his mother's death, his twenty-six-year-old brother, Edmund, a physician, died of scarlet fever, which he had contracted from one of his patients. Then came perhaps the greatest tragedy of all: the death of his father, whose example the future Pope would describe as "my first seminary."[11] Kneeling beside his father's body, he would recall, "I never felt so alone."[12]

Karol himself was hit by a truck in 1944 while a college student. Thrown onto the curb, he hit his head and lay unconscious. By divine providence, a German military officer picked up the young man and made sure he was taken care of at the nearest hospital. As an adult, the former sportsman was beset by physical difficulties, including a broken thigh that led to femur-replacement surgery, the removal of a precancerous tube from his colon, and a fall that led to a dislocated shoulder. Then, on May 13, 1981, the feast of Our Lady of Fatima, a bullet ripped into his stomach, right elbow, and left hand in St. Peter's Square. The Parkinson's disease that he later developed may well have been caused by the wounds. It is said that he missed death by a matter of millimeters. Even more remarkable are the x-rays that would reveal the trace of the bullet through the Pope's body, which formed the letter "M."

The Pope was to insert Alì Agca's assassination attempt within the "Marian thread" of his life: "This year, in a special way, after the attempt on my life, my conversation with Mary has been uninterrupted," he would later recount.[13] There was no doubt in the Pope's mind that the hand of Our Lady had guided and deflected the bullet. On the first anniversary of the shooting, the Pope traveled as a pilgrim to Fatima in gratitude to Mary for saving him. In his homily, he referred to the "mysterious coincidence"—that the attempt on his life had occurred on the anniversary of the first Fatima apparition.

Pope John Paul II is rightly known as "Mary's Pope" or the "most Marian Pope in history." It is also fitting that, like the Sorrowful Mother, he becomes known as "a man of suffering, accustomed to infirmity" (Is 53:3) who never ran away from the cross. As priests, the cross in our lives can mean loneliness, rejection, ridicule, and unjust accusations. Like Mary, who carried the "second" annunciation that "you yourself a sword will pierce" (Lk 2:35) all the way to the cross, Pope John Paul II would sometimes say, "never climb down from the cross, for Jesus never did."

In my work as assistant to the Holy Father for six synods, I witnessed how the cross was transformed into grace in his very person, for the weaker he grew, the more people of every walk of life found in him a consoling "witness of hope." Is it not fascinating that the Pope, who returned to the house of the Father on the feast of Divine Mercy, finishes his very last book, *Memory and Identity*, with the words from the prophet Isaiah: "By his stripes we are healed" (Is 53:5), imploring us to believe that "the limit imposed upon evil is Divine Mercy"?[14] May we, too, trust that our fruitfulness as priests will come through fidelity to the words spoken on our ordination day: "Model your life on the cross of Christ."

Saint Louis Marie de Montfort

How can we sit "At the School of the Mother"? Pope John Paul II recommends a concrete way. As a clandestine seminarian working in the Solvay soda plant in Kraków, Karol Wojtyla took up his spiritual director's advice to meditate on Saint Louis Marie de Montfort's spiritual classic, *True Devotion to the Blessed Virgin*. "Many times and with great spiritual profit I read and reread this precious little ascetic book, with the blue, soda-stained cover," the Pope remembers.[15] "The reading of the book was a decisive turning point in my life. . . . My devotion to Mary, modeled on this pattern, has lasted since then. It is an integral part of my inner life and my spiritual theology."[16] Indeed, in the Pope's episcopal arms, the motto *Totus tuus* takes its inspiration from the teaching of St. Louis Marie de Montfort. These words express total belonging to Jesus through Mary: "*Tuus totus ego sum, et omnia mea tua sunt,*" writes the saint, which he translates: "I am all yours and all I have is yours, O dear Jesus, through Mary, your holy Mother."[17]

One cannot understand Pope John Paul II's total gift of self without knowing something of the life and spirituality of Saint Louis Marie. In his first year after ordination, Father Louis Marie wrote to his spiritual director, describing his vocational objectives: "I feel a great desire to make Our Lord and His Holy Mother loved, and to go about in a poor and simple way, catechizing poor country people." In a life rooted in constant prayer, love of the poor, poverty carried to an unheard-of degree, and joy in humiliations and persecutions, this secular priest would spend his sixteen years in the Lord's vineyard doing just that, exhorting his own priests to preach with simplicity, truthfulness, without fear, and with charity, adding, "His intention must be holy and centered on God alone. God's glory must be his sole preoccupation, and he must first practice what he preaches."[18]

As a young man, Karol Wojtyla would discover through the saint's writing that the purpose of sound devotion to the Blessed Mother is to establish devotion to Jesus Christ more perfectly. Saint Louis Marie asserts that, when we give ourselves entirely into the maternal hands of Mary, she provides "a smooth but certain way of reaching Jesus Christ."[19] She is the one member of the human race who cooperated perfectly with God's grace. Satan, therefore, dreads her. For the Christian, the baptismal rejection of Satan and all his empty promises can be renewed in, with, and through Mary's maternal intercession, leading to an act of living faith in the Father, Son, and Holy Spirit.

For a priest, these two ends of Saint Louis Marie's "Consecration of Oneself to Jesus Christ, Eternal Wisdom, through the Blessed Virgin Mary"—death to sin and union with the life of the Blessed Trinity—are lived in very concrete ways. Death to sin involves the regular and sincere confession of sins, and careful practice of spiritual direction. As priests, we are led into union with the life of the

Blessed Trinity in a unique way through the Eucharist. Like the Mother of Jesus at the foot of the cross, each day at the altar we join our body to Jesus' sacrifice on Calvary for the redemption of the world: "This is my body, which will be given for you" (Lk 22:19). How important it is for us priests every day to celebrate the Eucharist and gaze upon the littleness and humility of Jesus in Eucharistic adoration.

But, above all, we need desire. Very early on in my priesthood, when I was experiencing a time of dryness, I asked Blessed Teresa of Calcutta personally: "How can I be holy?"

Her response has never left me. "If you have the desire," she told me, "God will do the rest." I may have achieved much in worldly terms through desire. But do I have the *desire to be holy*?

Let us sit at the school of Mary, our Mother, for she is the mold in which Jesus forms his saints. Pope John Paul II is living proof. St. Louis Marie's description of the "true Apostles of the latter times" fits our beloved Holy Father so well that I cannot but close with it, praying that just as Jesus had the humility to come to us through Mary, we may come to Jesus through Mary:

> But what will they be like, these servants, these slaves, these children of Mary?
>
> They will be ministers of the Lord who, like a flaming fire, will enkindle everywhere the fires of divine love. They will become in Mary's powerful hands, like sharp arrows, with which she will transfix her enemies.

They will be as children of Levi, thoroughly purified by the fire of great tribulations and closely joined to God. They will carry the gold of love in their heart, the frankincense of prayer in their mind and the myrrh of mortification in their body. They will bring to the poor and the lowly everywhere the sweet fragrance of Jesus. . . .

They will be true apostles of the latter times to whom the Lord of Hosts will give eloquence and strength to work wonders and carry off glorious spoils from his enemies. They will sleep without gold or silver and, more important still, without concern, in the midst of other priests, ecclesiastics and clerics. Yet they will have the silver wings of the dove enabling them to go wherever the Holy Spirit calls them, filled as they are with the resolve to seek the glory of God and the salvation of souls. . . .

Lastly, we know they will be true disciples of Jesus Christ, imitating his poverty, his humility, his contempt of the world and his love. . . . They will have the two-edged sword of the Word of God in their mouths and the blood-stained standard of the cross on their shoulders. They will carry the crucifix in the right hand and the rosary in their left, and the holy name of Jesus and Mary on their heart. The simplicity and self-sacrifice of Jesus will be reflected in their whole behavior.

Such are the great men who are to come. By the will of God Mary is to prepare them to extend his rule over the impious and unbelievers. But when and how will this come about? Only God knows. For our part we must yearn and wait for it in silence and prayer: "I have waited and waited."[20]

two

Mother of Every Priestly Grace

Rev. Msgr. Fernando Ferrarese

It was a windy, rainy night in mid-November. A chill accompanied the driving downpour. It was the kind of night that made you glad that you didn't have to go out. The rectory was empty. The other priests were out, and even the young man who worked in the office called in sick. My two appointments had cancelled, and I was looking forward to a quiet evening, catching up on my reading.

The phone rang, and a distraught parishioner named Mercedes asked if she could see me. She and her husband had been trying to conceive, and she was finally pregnant with her first child. On the phone, she was crying and needed to see me immediately. I told her that I was free and to come right over.

When she arrived, I was surprised that her husband had not come with her. She was drenched. I got her a towel and escorted her into my office. After a few casual remarks about the inclement weather, she sat down and told me the sad story of her recent miscarriage and the tension this introduced into her marriage. She spoke about her pain and how the loss seemed unbearable. Even though she was an educated, professional woman, there was something elemental and almost primitive in her response. She seemed inconsolable. I tried to respect her silences and stammered a few words of comfort that seemed to fall lifeless to the ground. Being both a representative of God and a man made me feel oddly ineffectual.

But then it happened. My mind thought of Mary and her pain at the loss of her Son. I prayed for her intercession. I began to talk to Mercedes about Our Lady and the fact that Mary understood what she was feeling. As I was encouraging her to confide in this special, loving woman, I felt a presence enter my office, a presence of ineffable sweetness. Like a fragrance that gradually permeates a room, this soft unseen person was simply "here" with us. As I spoke of Mary's courage, her abandonment to God at the cross, and of her love, Mercedes' weeping stopped, and a quiet peace stole into her face's grim hardness. The experience was real and perceptible, palpable for both of us.

Mercedes left after talking for another hour. As she re-entered the stormy night, she turned and gave me a look filled with gratitude. I felt that I had done nothing. I had merely received a great grace. This grace came in the form of a simple revelation: *Mary was real*.

I begin my reflections on Our Lady with this experience because much that is written about Mary tends to make her a symbol or part of a larger myth. Depending on whom you read, she is made to represent the femininity of God, or she is emblematic of the Palestinian peasantry, or she is a point of unity among the Abrahamic religions or a cause of disunity for Christians.

While conceding some value in these approaches, my starting point in reflecting on Mary in my life as a priest is that she is a real person, and not primarily a theological argument or a symbol of liberation. She is my mother in the Spirit, and I am her son in Christ. Intellectualizing her place in the Church strikes me as beside the point and even a little disrespectful. It simply dehumanizes her.

As a priest, I have often felt her to be a role model. Of course, we must imitate Christ, but because of his divine nature, we can only do so up to a point. Mary is only human, and that is her glory. Jesus' human life can rightly be termed an "*imitatio Mariae.*" That indeed is high praise!

Like a great icon, she always leads me to her Son. She never remains central. With a gentle but firm hand, she points to her Jesus. After all, was he not flesh from her flesh? To posit a tension between devotion to her and adherence to Christ is to misread the story of the redemption. As you approach her, she becomes transparent, and it is her Son you see.

Dante expressed this so poignantly in the *Paradiso*:

> Look upon the face that is most likened
> unto Christ; for its brightness and no other,
> hath power to fit thee to see Christ (Canto
> XXXII).[1]

As Christ's genetic human matrix, Mary's physical resemblance to her Son is used by Dante as a symbol of her likeness to him in all things.

As a priest of almost thirty years, I find her to be an inspiring model for my ministry. She is such a corrective to the "messiah complex," which sometimes afflicts the ordained ministry. She is transparent, and in that humility I see great spiritual wisdom as I follow her Son as his priest.

To illustrate this, I would like to consider three key moments in her life on earth and how these moments enrich my priestly ministry.

Christbearing

The first moment is familiarly referred to as the Visitation. Pregnant with the Lord, she enters Elizabeth's house and is greeted with the words: "Most blessed are you among women, and blessed is the fruit of your womb. And how does this happen to me, that the mother of my Lord should come to me?" (Lk 1:42–43). This is one of the truly poetic moments in scripture: the young mother reaching out to minister to the elderly mother; the babies communicating in the womb; and the interplay of Elizabeth's humility with the humility of Mary, who can boast of all the Lord has done in her. In one painting I recall, John the Baptist is expressing his joy by playing a fiddle!

This is what I do as a priest. I carry Christ in my womb of faith, and I seek to communicate the joy of redemption. I preach a Magnificat of praise by allowing the Lord to use my life as an example for God's people.

I often become aware of a kind of "gestation period of faith" when, in prayer and reflection, silently, Christ grows within me. That fullness is what priests feel at their ordination when God selects them through the Church to be Christ-bearers to the world. It is not an accident that Mary has been seen as the ultimate contemplative. Her pondering in her heart the events of salvation, her silent witness, is similar to the priest's life of prayer that in solitude and often in loneliness makes present the reality of Christ.

I often go to monasteries, where the haste and noise have not gained control. There, I can nurture within me that spiritual presence that I share in my ministry: to the elderly man who feels despair creeping in on him and needs the light of Christ; to the confused teenager who feels so alone and so unloved and needs the companionship of Christ; to the brother priest who has squandered his priesthood and seeks the forgiveness of Christ.

It has always struck me as significant that no one told Mary to go to Elizabeth's aid. Although she could easily have stayed home, she knew that her cousin needed her. Even as a young woman, she did not think of her own pregnancy and her own comfort. She took the initiative, as she would also do at Cana. She reached out in love, for she carried love within her.

The priest and poet Gerard Manley Hopkins caught this Marian role in his poem, "The Blessed Virgin Compared to the Air We Breathe." An excerpt of the poem:

Of her flesh he took flesh:
He does take fresh and fresh,
Though much the mystery how,
Not flesh but spirit now
And makes, O marvelous!
New Nazareths in us,
Where she shall yet conceive
Him, morning, noon and eve;
New Bethlehems, and be born
There, evening, noon and morn—
Bethlehem or Nazareth,

Men here may draw like breath
More Christ and baffle death;
Who, born so, comes to be
New self and nobler me
In each one and each one
More makes, when all is done,
Both God's and Mary's Son.[2]

Hopkins images the ongoing mystery of the incarnation: the fact that we are all called in our own uniqueness to bring forth Christ, and in so doing, become more our true selves in him, "New self and nobler me."

As a priest, I have found that the whole point of ministry is to help people make contact with their true selves. We are prisoners of our false selves, the masks we have inherited or chosen that we don't even know are there. To become authentic is to discover Christ. This is the mystery of Baptism, that daily sacrament that is at the heart of Pauline theology. To die to our former selves is to live in Christ. "For me to live is Christ, and death is gain" (Phil 1:21).

Like Mary, I carry the forming Word, and bring that emerging meaning to people in my daily life. I do this primarily through my own humanity, which "selves" Christ in my unique way. This humanity is what God has ordained. In the gestation of solitude and prayer, I try to image being brought forth in new "Bethlehems." But I do this as a public witness, his priest, so that this can happen in the more private spheres of my parishioners' lives.

I have found that when people make the connection that the life of Christ is within them, they feel a liberating energy that makes even the most difficult moral demands a joyful gift to God.

Compassionate Solidarity

The second Marian moment that has had formative power on my priestly service is that of Mary at the foot of the cross: "*Stabat Mater.*" In innumerable paintings, we see this most human of all moments: the powerless witnessing of a loved one's suffering. In John's gospel, the Lord says that when he is lifted up, he would draw all to himself. One of the ways to interpret this saying is that the Lord is talking about being lifted up on the cross. How accurate and realistic of Christ to see this as binding every human being on earth. For the experience of suffering is a common denominator for everyone.

I saw this clearly when I visited Mexico City. I was praying in an old church. In the corner was a particularly gruesome image of the crucified Christ. Nothing was left to the imagination. One could barely look at the figure. But in front of the crucifix was an old Mexican woman. The poverty present in that vast city could be clearly seen in her dress and weather-beaten face. She had her hands outstretched in prayer, a rosary dangling from one hand, her eyes transfixed by the broken man on the cross. In an instant, I intuited what the Lord meant. He draws all of us to himself in his suffering, for we all know what that is. That woman knew that she prayed to a God who understood all the pains and indignities of her life. That he was a man of sorrows, acquainted with pain.

Some spiritual writers speak of Mary's martyrdom. True, she was never executed like most of her Son's friends. But is not watching the suffering of others sometimes worse than suffering ourselves? Who among us has not powerlessly watched the suffering of loved ones?

I remember making my rounds at a local hospital and being asked by the pastoral minister to go into the pediatrics ward to be with a young couple. They had one child, about eighteen months old. I am not sure what his sickness was, but the upshot of it was that his head had grown to twice its normal size. It was bitterly painful and for some reason the doctors could not give the child painkillers. So the child writhed and cried, unable even to lift his head. He simply moved from one end of the crib to the other propelled by the pain that would not leave him. He whimpered and moaned and called for his mother. They were instructed not to pick him up. Perhaps it would have made the pain worse. His mother stood watching, her eyes red with crying. Her husband stood behind her, with his arm around her. They seemed so forlorn, so lost, beyond comfort or anger. They only wanted the pain to stop.

I walked in with that fearful powerlessness that every priest knows. They looked at me with a plea in their eyes, afraid to hope again. I prayed that I would not say something that would make their pain worse. I begged God for a miracle. But none happened. All I could do was watch with them. After a few questions, a reading, and a prayer, I gave the child my blessing as I did for his parents. I walked out like a guilty man.

The next day they were not there. The child had been transferred to another hospital. I have thought of that day often. It helps me to understand the depth of Mary's sorrow on Calvary. How much care she had taken to nurture him, to heal his bruises, to stay up with him when he had a fever. To see what they did to him must have been over-whelming. But she stood there still.

A priest sees a lot of suffering, and sometimes he can only stand there and pray. Christ had the power to heal by curing. The healing that a priest does is closer to the way Mary heals: by silent witness and compassion.

I remember a talk given by a priest who was a member of AA. He used the expression, "compassionate solidarity heals." Sometimes a priest can only extend the arms of his understanding and feel the pain of others. It is in that silent witness of solidarity and compassion that God heals the world.

Centering Faithfulness

Whenever you see a painting of Pentecost, Mary is in the very center. She is the present reminder of her Son and the promise of the future in the gift of the Holy Spirit. It was the Holy Spirit that overshadowed her in the conception of the Lord. Throughout her life, she responded to the promptings of that Spirit until the prophesied sword of sorrow on Calvary.

After the death, resurrection, and ascension of Jesus, she must have been a very reassuring presence to the early Church. She was the living tradition of faith and one who, by simply being, continued to magnify the Lord. She was stability in a world where the doors and windows fly open, tongues of flame descend, and mere fishermen and unlettered workman go forth to preach, to die, and to change the world.

I have been a pastor in two parishes. In both, I have sensed this role of stabilizer in a world that seems to be out of control, a still point in the whirlwind. There is a changelessness to the priesthood and to the Christian life, a sense of order and purpose that will outlast the most brutal and destructive attacks. The gates of hell, says the Lord, will not prevail.

This was brought home to me powerfully on Tuesday, September 11, 2001. I was assigned as the pastor of St. Athanasius parish in Brooklyn. Like most priests, my day started like any other day. But as the attack progressed and the devastation became apparent, we all realized that we would never be the same again. I recall having to go to the school to talk to the children. The school was in lockdown, and not even the teachers knew why. As I crossed the parking lot, the air was filled with falling ash, delicately descending like snow. It clung to me and coated the cars. Who could have known that the remains of the innocent were falling onto a new and more anguished world?

We decided, like most parishes, to open the church and to plan for an evening Eucharist that was obviously unannounced. We simply wanted to pray with the prayer of Jesus' self-sacrifice to the Father.

The church was packed, as people seemed drawn by a deep summons to pray. Instinctively, we all knew we had to be there. As I mounted the pulpit and looked into the stunned, needy eyes of my people, I never felt more a priest. They were coming to the church because it was only in the communion of faith that all this sorrow could be absorbed and transformed into hope. I don't know where the words came from, but they did. We all left the church knowing that faith is, in the end, the greatest reality of our lives. In talking to other priests, I know that my experience was common. The title, "Pastor of Souls" never seemed more apt.

Like Mary in the moment of Pentecost, a priest is that loving center that tries to speak the words of gospel truth and remind the people of God of what is most important in life. Like Mary, we help to draw the lessons of virtue from life's absurdity and share the gospel of life in this all-too-sad culture of death. And in so many ways! Whether it is the large family trying to make ends meet, the old person living alone, or the kindergarten tyke with the big theological questions, they look to the priest for that sense of integrating purpose that makes sense of things, even when things do not make sense.

Mary is quite real to me. Whether in Elizabeth's house, on Calvary, or in the Cenacle, Mary has been a model in my priesthood. Some of the most beautiful pages ever written about Our Lady can be found in Georges Bernanos's *Diary of a Country Priest.* Like the *curé* in the book, I long to see her of whom he writes:

> Our Lady knew neither triumph nor miracle. Her Son preserved her from the last tip-touch of the savage wing of human glory. No one has ever lived, suffered, died in such simplicity, in such deep ignorance of her own dignity, a dignity crowning her above the Angels.[3]

three

Mary, the Pope, and the American Apostle of the Family Rosary

Rev. Willy Raymond, C.S.C.

One day in 1994, I received a call to the bedside of Mr. LeBlanc, a gravely ill gentleman whom I knew to be a man of deep and genuine faith. In the hospital room where he lay dying, his adult daughter, son, and the son's wife surrounded him with love and attention. Following the Anointing of the Sick and Viaticum, he requested the reading of some prayers from scripture. Although clearly in pain and dying, he was beaming with joy, and, in a barely audible voice, chanted softly, "Alleluia." In a poignant moment of stillness between prayers, he suddenly began to share with his children and me the reason for his joy. He said, "I can see someone coming toward me—she is the most beautiful woman I have ever seen, and I think I know who she is." He then said, "There are many others with her." At this, his daughter stroked his arm gently and whispered, "Dad, if you wish to go with them, please go. We know now that you are going to something wonderful. Don't worry about us; we will be fine." A few moments later he slipped away with great joy and peace.

Walking from the hospital to the parking lot on a late New England winter afternoon—it was nearly dusk—I paused a moment, took a deep breath of fresh cold air, and thanked God. He had allowed me to have a rare glimpse of grace and holiness working in a person, as if beyond time and space and at the threshold of eternity. I had just shared a father's personal account of the presence of the Mother of God, in all her grace and comeliness, greeting him with his relatives behind her and the familiar saints he knew, and leading him to her Son. Outside the Eucharist, this is the closest I have come to an experience of heaven on earth. The poet Gerard Manley Hopkins compared Mary to the "air we breathe," as if her very graceful presence was somehow akin to the atmosphere that surrounds us. As I exhaled the crisp winter air that afternoon, I knew I would forever cherish this moment of grace. I had experienced Mary's rarified air of grace blessed in the alleluia of a dying man.

Mary has been a fact of my life for as long as I can remember. In my earliest childhood memory, I can recall the voice of my mother speaking with Mary in French—she kneeling, her head resting in her hands, her rosary beads dangling from her fingers, praying, *"Je vous salue, Marie, pleine de grâce, le Seigneur est avec vous. . . ."* For most of my formative years, my parents gathered their twelve children each evening after supper to pray the rosary. The recollection of those evenings of long ago continues to support and animate my own faith in God and devotion to Mary.

When I joined the Congregation of Holy Cross in 1964 as a twenty-year-old college student, Vatican II was in progress, and developments from Rome frequently made front-page news. As a novice and young professed religious, the rosary was a daily devotion prayed both in common and in private. Mary, Our Lady of Sorrows, was and still remains the patroness of Holy Cross. The plaintive Salve Regina was sung by heart at the conclusion of Compline and often after the rosary. The cult of Mary figured large in Holy Cross as it has in the Church throughout much of her history. In some centuries, Mary's appeal seemed to overwhelm the Holy Trinity and the Word of God made flesh, at least in the popular mind.

Joseph Campbell called Notre Dame de Chartres, "The parish church of the world." This most captivating of churches deeply impressed Henry Adams, the grandson and great-grandson of two American presidents. He speaks of the glory and grandeur of devotion to Mary at its high-water mark in the thirteenth century:

> The church is wholly given up to the Mother and the Son. The Father seldom appears; the Holy Ghost still more rarely. At least this is the impression made on an ordinary visitor who has no motive to be orthodox; and it must have been the same with the thirteenth-century worshipper who came here with his mind absorbed in the perfections of Mary. Chartres represents, not the Trinity, but the identity of the Mother and Son. The Son represents the Trinity, which is thus absorbed in the Mother. The idea is not orthodox, but this is no affair of ours. The Church watches over its own.[1]

At Vatican II the Church desired to make right the relationship of Mary to God, to the Trinity, and to the Church. But even Mother Church seemed to lose control in the tumultuous days of the late 1960s following Vatican Council II. Mary and the rosary, her images and statues, her hymns and novenas, disappeared almost overnight from seminaries, churches, and theological studies, as if to leave the faithful with only a fond remembrance of her. The much heralded renewal of Catholic life stressed the centrality of Christ and the Eucharist, of word and sacrament. As Walter Burghardt says: "We may well have succeeded in subordinating rosary to liturgy, Mary to Mass and mother to Son."[2] My own experience as a seminarian and young priest internalized this movement away from Marian devotions in much of the Catholic world, though not all.

Two figures, however, have helped reinvigorate my personal devotion to Mary and the rosary. The first was the Polish pontiff elected in 1978, who bravely announced to the whole world his confidence in Mary with the asymmetrical "M" on a blue field on his coat of arms, and who proclaimed as his motto, *Totus Tuus*, "All Yours, Mary." At every turn he invoked Our Lady, whom he believed to have saved his life on that fateful May 13, 1981. He concluded all of his official teaching documents by entrusting the Church and his petrine ministry to her maternal care. More importantly, he skillfully and beautifully presented the right order of devotion to Mary and the saints in service to worship of the one God, Father, Son, and Holy Spirit, in *Rosarium Virginis Mariae*. Mary is clearly subordinate to God and, in the "School of Mary," she takes disciples by the hand and leads them through the great mysteries of the life of Christ. Pope John Paul's addition of the five

Luminous Mysteries to the traditional fifteen makes the rosary even more clearly a Christocentric devotion. As a young bishop at Vatican II, he actively participated in the deliberations that crafted its constitutions and decrees. He knew that Vatican II had gotten the relationship of Mary to the Church and God just right. As Scott Hahn writes: "The Church discussed this in a dazzling way in the documents of the Second Vatican Council (1962–1965). Though this council produced no single document focused exclusively on Mary, its documents as a whole included more Marian teaching than any other ecumenical council in Church history. In fact, the Marian teaching of Vatican II outweighed that of all previous councils combined."[3]

The second figure that helped reinvigorate my devotion to Mary is the late Father Patrick Peyton, C.S.C., who died in 1992. He, like Pope John Paul II, was at Vatican II and intimately involved in helping to shape the Church's thinking and teaching about Mary. He was delighted at the length and quality of the Council's Constitution on the Church, *Lumen Gentium*, and the role of Mary detailed in Chapter VIII. The Council viewed Mary as "Mother of the Church" (LG 54) and the Christian home as a "domestic Church" (LG 11). Father Peyton lobbied cardinals, bishops, and even the Pope, to make sure that the Council covered this important territory. He is now called "Servant of God" and is a candidate for sainthood. Because of his importance on the American Catholic scene and in my own life as a priest working in Hollywood at Family Theater Productions, which he founded, I would like to devote some space in this short essay to this priest and his spirituality.

In 2003, the Archdiocese of San Francisco celebrated 150 years of dramatic history. In that century and a half there had been gold rushes, earthquakes, the construction of the Golden Gate Bridge and the Bay Bridge, the dedication of a new cathedral, the assassination of a mayor, World Series and NFL championships, and a visit by Pope John Paul II. None of these gained first place as the most significant event in the history of the archdiocese. According to the archivist of the Archdiocese of San Francisco, that distinction went to the October 7, 1961, Family Rosary Crusade Rally for which more than 500,000 people crammed into Golden Gate Park. They came to pray together and to hear the powerful message of Father Peyton: "The family that prays together stays together," and "A world at prayer is a world at peace."

Who was this man, and why did so many millions hunger to hear his message? The late actress Loretta Young responded to this question in a pellucidly clear statement: "I never knew a man who loved a woman more than Father Peyton loved Our Blessed Mother."[4]

Fortunately, Father Peyton, in radio interviews and in his autobiography *All for Her,* spoke with passion and self-disclosure about the foundations of his Marian spirituality and his priestly vocation. In Father Peyton's own words:

> I was born on January 9, 1909, in a picturesque valley of County Mayo. On one side were the Ox Mountains and on the other the Atlantic Ocean.
>
> From my earliest memories, I saw my father with the rosary beads in his hands and my mother holding hers. My older brothers and sisters and I knelt around them, praying. My father began with the Sign of the Cross, then the Apostles' Creed, the Our Father's, the Hail

Mary's, the Glory Be's. What impressed me most was the voice of my mother talking to Mary: "Holy Mary, Mother of God, pray for us sinners now and at the hour of our death. Amen!"

For the first nineteen years of my life this was our daily practice as I grew from childhood, to boyhood, to my teens. In good times and in bad, in sickness and in health, in poverty and hard work, we ended each day speaking to Jesus and his Mother, offering them the greatest tribute that could possibly be given, making the greatest act of faith, and honoring Mary above all the angels and saints. Because of the daily family rosary, my home was for me a cradle, a school, a university, a library, and most of all, a little church.

In May 1928, my brother and I emigrated to Scranton, Pennsylvania to join our three sisters. A day or two before we left him forever, my father asked me to kneel before a picture of the Sacred Heart. He addressed Our Lord with an intensity from his heart as he entrusted me completely to his care and protection. Then he said words, which were engraved on my heart: "Be faithful to Our Lord in America." At the railway station I saw my mother for the last time. She waved her handkerchief until the train disappeared from sight. My heart was crushed with sorrow, and tears blinded my eyes.

Not in our wildest imaginings did my parents or my brother or I dream what Our Lord had in store for us in America. He called my brother to the priesthood from the coal mines of Scranton. He called me from being the janitor in Saint Joseph's Cathedral. In the fall of 1929 we entered the seminary at Notre Dame, Indiana. There we continued the family rosary with our new family, the priests and seminarians of Holy Cross.

Two years before my ordination I was stricken with a serious illness. I was forced to leave the seminary. At the infirmary at Notre Dame, I learned the three lessons that have directed me on my journey.

The first lesson was my total dependence on my neighbor—the doctors, the nurses, and their assistants. How I learned that famous line from literature: "No man is an island." We are all one family, all one in Christ, all members of his body. We form with him a "Mystical Body" that is closer even than the branches and the leaves of a tree are to the trunk that gives them life.

The second lesson was about the precious gift of Jesus' mother, given with his dying breath on the cross. In the infirmary I deteriorated until the doctors said, "Try prayer, our remedies are useless." One of my former teachers heard the bad news and hurried to visit me. He saw me at my worst—discouraged, depressed, hopeless.

His words were the most important ever spoken to me. "Mary is alive," he said. "She will be as good to you as you think she can be. It all depends on you and your faith."

That night, he activated my dormant faith. It was like setting a match to a haystack sprinkled with gasoline. Thanks to the family that always prayed the rosary, I had come to know who Mary was and that Jesus Christ, her Son, had entrusted me to her love and care. I asked her with all my heart and soul to pray to her Son for my cure.

Like the dark night that is replaced by dawn and the dawn by the sun, she brought me back to life. I was certain Our Blessed Mother was taking part in my healing. I am not describing a miracle. I am giving witness to the power of Mary's intercession and the quiet, unsensational way she works. I begged the doctors to examine me once more and received their report in a letter. Like a prisoner waiting for the verdict of the jury, I opened the letter and saw my freedom, my new lease on life, my second spring.

The first words I spoke were, "Mary, I hope I never disgrace you." My superiors sent me back to the seminary. On June 15, 1941, I knelt beside my brother in Sacred Heart Church on the campus of Notre Dame and was made a priest. I remembered my father's words on seeing the photograph of us both wearing priests' garments: "I cry with joy to see what God has done for our two boys."

How could I pay back my debts to our Lord, his Mother, and my family? I prayed for an answer. Seven months after my ordination, while on retreat, God gave me the answer—the Family Rosary Crusade.

It was frightening! It was impossible! How could I do it? I spoke these words to Our Lord in a small chapel: "I can't do it. But, My Lord, you can, and I ask you to do it." It was the best prayer I ever uttered. *I had learned my third lesson: Without God, I can do nothing.* I took that lesson to heart. And God answered me in a way I would never have dreamed.[5]

Father Peyton then describes his use of the mass media to spread his message of prayer, family unity, and the rosary. He became a media pioneer in Hollywood on radio, television, and film. He befriended hundreds of Hollywood actors, writers, directors, and producers. He became a master at begging for help from supporters of both great and modest means everywhere. He used his growing celebrity status to organize rosary rallies around the world in a great, ongoing, global crusade to save the family by linking it to family prayer and the rosary, the glue that would hold the family together. Over the decades, more than twenty-eight million people participated in the rosary rallies in gatherings of hundreds of thousands and, in some cases, millions.

The Hollywood actor and Catholic convert, Clarence Gilyard, from the television series *Matlock* and *Walker*,

Texas Ranger, frequently responds to the pedestrian greeting, "How are you?" with the refreshing refrain, "I am blessed." Blessed is the word I would use for two brief interviews I had with young priests for this essay. Both reside in a rectory they share with five other priests, including myself. Both are effective ministers of word and sacrament and much loved and admired by their parishioners.

One is a Vietnamese-American in his early forties, ordained eight years. He came to this country as a teenager with his mother and sister after surviving a perilous journey by boat from his homeland. When I asked him what role Mary played in his life and spirituality, he responded eagerly: "She is the reason I entered the seminary and became a priest." He shared that Mary was and is important, especially for the Vietnamese; and that he used to pray with her in mind, and she helped direct him to the seminary and priesthood. He also stated that Mary continues to be a major influence in his life as the Mother of Christ and Mother of the Church, and also as the first and best disciple of Jesus.

The second interview was with a young Ghanaian in his early thirties who lives in the same rectory and has been a priest for six years. He is in residence at this parish and in his second year of graduate studies in pastoral theology. When the same question was put to him, he responded emphatically, "She is the Mother. How can I not love and respect her?" His devotion to Mary and her importance in his life and spirituality are clear and explicit.

Having never discussed Mary with either priest before, I was pleasantly surprised and encouraged by the healthy relationship these two promising young men have with Mary. The recovery of the practice of daily rosary has cleared a helpful path for me into the life of Christ seen through the eyes of the one who knew him best and loved him most: his mother. There is a small aide that I frequently turn to called *Father Peyton's Rosary Prayer Book*. It serves me and many others well because it uses a simple, three-step formula for praying each of the mysteries. These include: (1) a relevant line from scripture, (2) a brief spiritual/theological reflection on the mystery, and (3) immediate, personal application in prayer. I use the Luminous Mystery, "The Wedding Feast at Cana," to illustrate:

> (1) "His mother said to the servers, 'Do whatever he tells you'" (Jn 2:5).

> (2) In the wedding feast of Cana, Mary takes the initiative in the ministry of her Son. She tells the servants, "Do whatever he tells you." Mary, the Mother of the Church, is telling us the same. What it means to be a follower of Jesus as Church is contained in his pilgrimage of ministry. Mary tells us to preach, heal, love, and sacrifice as he did. As difficult as that may seem, following him in his Church is the only way to freedom. We must do whatever he tells us.

> (3) "Loving Christ, may I come to you often in prayer, alone and with other members of the Church in order to discern what it is you want me to do."[6]

Allow me to conclude with the remarkably pertinent prayer of the master teacher now occupying the Chair of Peter:

Holy Mary, Mother of God,
you have given the world its true light,
Jesus, your Son—the Son of God.
You abandoned yourself completely
to God's call
and thus became a wellspring
of the goodness which flows forth from him.
Show us Jesus. Lead us to him,
teach us to know and love him
so that we too can become
capable of true love
and be fountains of living water
in the midst of a thirsting world.[7]

four

Mary, Mother of God and Mother of the Church, Walks with Her Son's Priests

Rev. Louis J. Cameli

One of my earliest memories is of my mother teaching me the Hail Mary and explaining a picture of the Blessed Mother in a book of prayers. The memory has stayed with me. The sense of Mary's presence in my life that began in that moment has stayed with me as well. As a child, I did not know or fully appreciate that Mary, the mother of Jesus, would be a steady and faithful companion to me on my spiritual journey. In retrospect, it makes all the sense in the world. As I studied theology and, more particularly, spirituality, I understood the *communio sanctorum* and Mary's privileged place in that great communion. I can clearly say that she has walked with me as my faith life has unfolded. She has been a most extraordinary companion in the course of my priestly ministry and life.

As a student of contemporary Catholic spirituality, I have come to know the importance of accompaniment on the spiritual journey. The Catholic tradition strongly emphasizes that our spiritual lives do not unfold in a private or individualistic way.[1] We go to God together. We accompany each other as members of the Body of Christ, the pilgrim People of God, the communion of saints.

Accompaniment means that we learn from each other and that we support one another. All of us are bound together by the same Holy Spirit whom the Lord sends into our hearts. The Holy Spirit inspires mutual teaching and reciprocal support in the Church.

Catholic tradition insists, and my experience confirms, that a preeminent companion for all Christians on our journey of faith that leads to the Father's house is the Blessed Virgin Mary.[2] This great and humble woman is overshadowed by the Holy Spirit and gives birth to Jesus Christ, the Word made flesh. She is the first and most perfect disciple of her Son. From the cross, Jesus gives her to all disciples as their Mother. And she collaborates with the Holy Spirit in teaching disciples how to follow her Son and in encouraging them on the challenging journey that discipleship entails. Not surprisingly, she serves her Son's followers in specific ways that correspond to their particular vocations in the Church. For this reason, we can securely affirm that she is a caring mother who teaches and encourages the priests who serve in the Church and who serve by acting in the name and person of Jesus Christ. She keeps them focused on who they are and what they are to do for the sake of their mission and the communion with God that is our shared destiny. She gives them encouragement along the way.

In my own priestly ministry and life, I have discovered certain "stations" or focal points of Mary's life that have provided me with a key for understanding the exact nature of my ministry and life as a priest and, at the same time, a way of receiving encouragement as I strive to stay faithful to my calling and service. I want to share these stations in Mary's life and illustrate what they have meant for me as a priest. As I do so, I am very much aware that the realities I indicate are alive, right now among us in the communion of saints. Both as believers and as priests, we have access to her whom Jesus Christ has given to us as mother, teacher, and source of hope.

Fiat: Let It Be Done

I know of no other group of men who are so willing, even anxious, to help other people as priests. It is in our bones to want to help others, especially those in need. So often, we desperately want to do something for our people, even when we know that there is very little that can be done. Just the other day, I was with a young wife who sat by her husband's bedside in a hospital. He is dying of cancer. She is bearing the burden of his illness, her impending loss, and the grief of their only son who is completely attached to his father. I very much want to help, to do something that would make the situation better or, at least, easier to bear. I know that there is really nothing that I can do. I am drawn in this moment, as I often have been, to Mary at the Annunciation.

She says in reply to the angel Gabriel, "Here am I, the servant of the Lord, let it be done to me according to your word." In these few words from among the few words of

Mary that we find in the Bible, there is a density of meaning. I hear her say, "There is nothing I can do, nothing that I can give. I can only give myself. Here am I, the servant of the Lord. I can only make myself available to the divine purpose." In pronouncing her *fiat*, Mary gives and does everything necessary—the gift of herself. Her *fiat* will echo her Son's self-sacrificial and Eucharistic offering: "This is my body which will be given up for you."

The letter to the Hebrews speaks of Christ's sacrifice and cites Psalm 40:

When [Christ] came into the world, he said:
"Sacrifice and offering you did not desire,
   but a body you prepared for me;
holocausts and sin offerings you took no
   delight in.
Then I said, ". . . Behold, I come to do your will,
O God" (Heb 10:5–7).

In her *fiat*, Mary teaches priests the essential element of her Son's priestly offering and the path to follow for those who exercise priestly ministry today: the total and complete gift of self beyond the particulars of ministry or service to the community.[3] It is enough to give oneself, to make oneself available for God's purpose. The rest will follow. Of this we can rest assured, because we know from her who gave without reserve and enabled the Word to become flesh and dwell among us.

Magnificat: My Soul Magnifies the Lord

When Mary encounters her cousin Elizabeth, the graciousness of God surges from her heart and must find a voice in her great song of praise. "My soul proclaims the greatness of the Lord; my spirit rejoices in God my savior" (Lk 1:46–47). Mary teaches us that the great and gracious deeds of God must be proclaimed. This is already at work in the mind and heart of the psalmist:

> My mouth shall proclaim your just deeds,
> day after day your acts of deliverance,
> though I cannot number them all.
> I will speak of the mighty works of the Lord;
> O God, I will tell of your singular justice (Ps 71:15–16).

In her urgent proclamation of the great deeds of God, Mary teaches priests the meaning of their *primum officium*, their first task or responsibility. This is the preaching of the word, expressed by the Second Vatican Council in the Decree on the Ministry and Life of Priests as "the proclamation of the gospel to all" (MLP 4). Everything else in priestly ministry flows from this foundational event of proclamation. It is exactly what Saint Paul meant when he wrote: "'Everyone who calls on the name of the Lord shall be saved.' But how are they to call on one in whom they have not believed? And how are they to believe in one of whom they have never heard? And how are they to hear without someone to proclaim him? And how are they to proclaim him unless they are sent?" (Rom 10:13–15).

Every evening prayer, Mary's Magnificat—her heartfelt proclamation to Elizabeth and to the world of God's great and gracious actions—is on the lips of priests. This prayer challenges and encourages us to engage in proclaiming the saving work of God in Jesus Christ by the power of the Holy Spirit. At the end of the day, can we say that we have let the world know the saving power of God's love manifest in Jesus Christ? As we voice Mary's words, are we one with her in sensing the urgency that every grace given must be expressed and proclaimed? As we look back upon a day, have we been so enmeshed in particular problems or concerns that the saving grace of God has eluded us and, therefore, have we been silent about what matters most?

Daily, Mary encourages us who exercise priestly ministry to shape our activities, our investments of time and energy, and even our preoccupations around an insistent proclamation of the mighty deeds of God in Jesus Christ in the power of the Holy Spirit. To absorb this lesson and this encouragement from the Mother of the Lord is to find our lives and energies realigned—and all that in the direction of conformity with God's will.

Epiphania: He Was Revealed in Flesh

Embedded with Mary in the infancy narratives is a paradigm of all priestly ministry, especially for priests who serve in parishes. When the Wise Men arrive in Bethlehem, St. Matthew says, "On entering the house, they saw the child with Mary his mother . . ." (Mt 2:11). Similarly, St. Luke speaks of the shepherds, ". . . they went with haste and found Mary and Joseph, and the infant lying in the manger" (Lk 2:16).

It is the *epiphania* of the Lord, his shining out, his manifestation, in this world and to all peoples. It is, at the same time, Mary his mother who holds him out and toward the world, so that he may be manifest and cast his light on those who have walked in the shadow of death. She makes no distinctions, whether they are highly educated foreign guests who bring gold, or local shepherds of low estate who bring only themselves. Her Son is for everyone, and she is solicitous to share him with everyone.

When I am in the vestibule after Sunday Mass, I am caught in an amazing swirl of people who speak many different languages, many of whom are immigrants from distant places. There is the span of ages that ranges from babes in arms to nonagenarians who are blessedly determined to go to Mass, at all costs! I am bold enough to be there for all of them, trying to speak a common language of faith and striving to make Jesus Christ the cord that binds them all together in their diversity. It seems to be an impossible task.

Mary teaches me and encourages me that it is possible to bring her Son to all these different people. It is enough to hold him out and toward them whether in preaching or sacramental celebration, or in a simple human gesture. Once he is presented, he will manifest himself according to God's purpose. He will shine out. He will be the light for everyone. His epiphany as Lord of all is hindered neither by my limitations nor the complex diversity of those whom he has come to save. He shines out before them, inevitably like the sun, for he is the dawn from on high.

Contemplatio: Treasuring All These Things in Her Heart

As St. Luke recounts the Holy Family's two journeys to the Temple in Jerusalem, both for the presentation of Jesus and for the celebration of the Passover, they begin as ordinary events of ritual observance. As they unfold, however, they become mysterious, inscrutable, even hurtful events that leave Mary and Joseph wondering. The final description of Mary's response is unexpected and utterly instructive. St. Luke says, "His mother kept all these things in her heart" (Lk 2:51). It is hardly surprising that when human beings encounter divine purpose, there is puzzlement and perhaps even deep confusion. God speaking through the prophet Isaiah says, "For my thoughts are not your thoughts, nor are your ways my ways, says the LORD" (Is 55:8). What is surprising and instructive is Mary's response. It is a contemplative response in the face of the mystery of the Word made flesh unfolding among us. She treasured all these things in her heart.

In the course of serving as priests, we inevitably encounter not only our own puzzlement, but also the often intense questioning of the people we serve. Of course, when we stand at the intersection of the holy mystery of God and human response to that mystery—as we do on a daily basis as priests—there should be no surprise that we share a common befuddlement with our people. The circumstances in which this happens are many: facing grief, dealing with illness, experiencing success, choosing a life direction, confronting human anger, engaging human and divine love. The list is endless. The puzzlement is similar and, often, very intense.

There is an almost gravitational pull within us to try and figure out what is happening, to determine what this all means, and to identify causes, factors, and outcomes. It is a highly rational response to the mystery of God alive in our priestly ministry. Especially as men, we are highly susceptible to this approach. Mary shows us a different way.

When she treasures things in her heart, she assumes a contemplative stance. She watches and waits. She does not try to figure things out. She is confident that God's truth will emerge. She instructs us by her example. We only need alert attention and patient waiting. God's truth will come to the surface.

Fuga Mundi: Flight From the World

When hostile forces threaten to devour and destroy her Son, Mary resists by fleeing with him and Joseph to Egypt (Mt 2:14). When she takes flight from a world of threatening violence, Mary does not react passively. On the contrary, she goes with Joseph in virtue of a deliberate and active decision. They will not engage evil on its own terms. They will wait for the opportune moment and then—and only then—return home.

Mary's pattern of response has much to say to us who serve as priests. Many of us, raised and formed in what we later assessed to be an anti-humanist environment and mindset, reacted by embracing uncritically a world that is still marked by sin. We have perhaps been naive about the effects of evil and residue of sin at work in the world. Mary's realism is a healthy antidote to this uncritical view, and it helps to disabuse us of our naiveté.

There is struggle; there is evil. To serve as a priest inevitably leads us to encounter a realm of darkness that threatens to do violence to us and to the people entrusted to us. What do we do with that? If we follow Mary's example, we begin with a clearheaded assessment of our situation.

We do not allow ourselves to be surprised or caught off guard by the existence of evil and hostile forces that work against the proclamation of the gospel. At the same time, we do not engage them on their own terms. We do so on God's terms. "Rise, take the child and his mother, flee to Egypt, and stay there until I tell you . . ." (Mt 2:13).

As she teaches us about dealing with evil, Mary encourages us. As the *Virgo assumpta*, the Virgin assumed into heaven, she remains a steady sign of Christ's triumph over darkness and his victory over the powers and the principalities.

Transformatio: He Changed Water into Wine

The wedding feast at Cana contains a *locus classicus* for devotion to Mary encapsulated in her words: "Do whatever he tells you" (Jn 2:5). Indeed, they are powerful words—words of encouragement that point us in a direction. Her simple directive tells us that she is a sure guide to her Son; whoever listens to her will certainly accomplish what Jesus wants.

There is another dimension to this story, one that also instructs and encourages us. It has special relevance for priests who are serving God's people. In the story of Cana, Mary facilitates and witnesses a miracle of transformation. Through her request that is framed as a fact, "They have no wine," through her direction given to the servants, "Do whatever he tells you," she enables her Son to work a marvelous transformation and so reveal his glory.

For reasons unknown to me, when I have had administrative responsibilities in a retreat house and now in a parish, boilers have broken down and bugged me. For me, they are the primordial symbols that keep reminding me of my responsibility to maintain the operation, something that I know I must do and something that I am committed to doing. When I watch Mary and listen to her at Cana, I also pray that I may not be stuck in the boilers.

As important as maintenance is, be it of a physical plant or a living congregation, even more important is the transformation that the Lord wants to work for his people. He wants to soften hearts, make enemies speak to one another, lift up the oppressed, redirect the energies of his disciples, create justice and peace; in a word, renew the face of the earth and all its inhabitants. Now we are not the agents of transformation. The Lord by the power of the Holy Spirit makes all things new. We do, however, collaborate and foster the process. I draw inspiration and encouragement from Mary, Mother of the Lord, at Cana. Here, I see simple gestures and quiet instructions that lead to great transformation and a revelation of Jesus' glory. I re-center myself, not neglecting what must be maintained, but also not forgetting the great work of transformation that lies ahead.

Juxta Crucem: She Stands by the Cross

When St. John describes Mary at the cross (Jn 19:26–27), he describes her as a teacher in the face of suffering and as a source of hope and comfort in life's most difficult moments. At the cross, she stands faithfully. Others have fled, are scattered in different directions. She remains. At the cross, she is the woman of compassion, literally, *com-passio*, suffering with her crucified Son. At the cross, she faces every challenge to hope and does so with the steadiness and courage that comes from her fundamental commitment: here am I, let it be done to me according to your word. At the cross, she moves beyond her personal grief to accept the grieving beloved disciple and every other follower of Jesus who bears heavy burdens.

Our ministry and life as priests do not exempt us from sharing in the mystery of the cross. In fact, we enter it more deeply—our own personal share, but also in the lives of the people entrusted to us. We do not always easily know what we are to do or how we are to be. It is a great grace to be taught what it means to stand by the cross by the mother of the crucified Lord. Simple, faithful presence is perhaps most often enough. A willingness to share in the sufferings of others is another way. A reaffirmation of our commitments in the face of whatever would diminish us or our people is yet another way. Beyond our own personal struggles, a community of disciples awaits our connection and our care, because the Lord entrusts them to us.

Our waiting with Mary at the foot of the cross instructs us and gives us hope. The end of our waiting comes, when, from the cross, he hands over his spirit (Jn 19:29) and from his side blood and water flow (Jn 19:34), and the Church is born and we are reborn.

In Medio Ecclesiae: In the Midst of the Church

Mary gathers with other disciples in the Upper Room (Acts 1:14). She sits waiting with them for the coming of the Holy Spirit. She is in the midst of the Church, remembering, interceding, and encouraging her Son's followers. She gave him a body, *ave verum corpus natum de Maria*, and now she cooperates again with the Holy Spirit in the formation of his mystical body, his Church.

Priests of Jesus Christ must stay steadily in the midst of the Church. They, too, must remember and intercede and encourage the followers of Jesus, until he comes again in glory. In the words of the Second Vatican Council, ". . . in the glory in the bodily and spiritual glory which she possesses in heaven, the Mother of Jesus continues in this present world as the image and first flowering of the Church as she is to be perfected in the world to come. Likewise Mary shines forth on earth, until the day of the Lord shall come (cf. 2 Pet 3:10), as a sign of sure hope and solace for the pilgrim People of God" (LG 68).

Gratias Agamus Domino Deo Nostro:
Let Us Give Thanks to the Lord Our God

Parishioners sometimes ask me, "Father, you must get lonely, don't you?" And I respond—to their puzzlement, I think—"No, not really." Solitude is something that I prize; and, at the same time, I have never felt a lack of genuine companionship. Friends have walked with me in the priesthood. The people I have served have been a strong and consoling presence in my life. And crowning it all is the company of Mary, the mother of the Lord, our great high priest. Her presence to me—and I hope that I have been able to communicate this adequately—is certainly consoling and encouraging. More than that, it nudges me and challenges me to greater conformity with her Son.

This great companion, this incalculable gift, leads me to the praise and thanksgiving of God. The words of Gerard Manley Hopkins in his poem, "The Blessed Virgin

Compared to the Air We Breathe" express for me the wonder of her companionship:

> . . . I say that we are wound
> With mercy round and round
> As if with air: the same
> Is Mary, more by name,
> She, wild web, wondrous robe,
> Mantles the guilty globe,
> Since God has let dispense
> Her prayers his providence. . . .[4]

five

Priests' Response in the Face of Reports of Marian Private Revelations

Rev. Benedict J. Groeschel, C.F.R.

Among the many taxing challenges a bishop or pastor may face is the unsettling news that Our Lady is reported to have been seen in the diocese or parish. Perhaps it is fear that generally prompts a negative, if not hostile, response among the clergy to news of apparitions or private revelations. Despite the fact that Saint Bernadette or the children at Fatima may be depicted in the church or on the parish grounds, most clergy do not take contemporary reports, even those with some Church approval, with anything remotely approaching enthusiasm. One reason is that a large majority of such claims and reports are found to be without substance. Some, moreover, are obviously linked to serious psychological illness. Another reason, less often recognized, is that if a supernatural event has occurred, it is clearly not under the control of the clergy, the parish council, or the diocesan authorities. If a report turns out to be true, Our Lady has, so to speak, trumped the deck. The only thing left for the clergy to do is to be chaplains or caretakers of the multitudes that will come.

Several years ago I wrote a book about the Church's guidelines for reports of the supernatural. When I was asked to contribute to this volume, therefore, I thought that a practical chapter on Church teaching and policy might be helpful. While a priest may never have to deal directly with a sincere person who believes that a supernatural event has occurred to him or her, he may well encounter many people who are highly interested in and enthusiastic about reports of apparitions and revelations.

In *A Still, Small Voice*, I tried to give logical steps and norms for evaluating and assisting someone who believes sincerely that he or she has received a direct message from Our Lady, Our Lord or, occasionally, a saint.[1] Most of us are unaware that there is a standard classic work on this subject: *The Graces of Interior Prayer* by Father Augustin Poulain, S.J.[2] I have tried to summarize Father Poulain's authoritative teaching in contemporary language. His chapters on extraordinary phenomena and unusual religious experiences range from inspired writings and locutions to the stigmata.

When an apparently sane person reports such phenomena, the first thing to do, obviously, is to read what you can and get plenty of advice. Simply dismissing a sincere and devout person can be seen at best as defensive and at worst as neglect of duty. Since the vast majority of these events are not authentic gifts of God, according to no less an authority than Saint John of the Cross, the person who is sincere but mistaken may be seriously hurt if treated with disdain and then dismissed.

A much more frequent challenge to pastoral skills is handling the enthusiasm of those who are intrigued or even mesmerized by a report of a private revelation. For example, we all know sane and sophisticated people whose lives have been changed by the events reported at Medjugorje, even in the face of the local bishop's negative assessment. Is there an intelligent and responsible way to guide fervent Catholics, and even non-Catholics, who are convinced that these reports are authentic occurrences, of supernatural origin, related to the intervention of the Mother of God from the reality of the next world?

Some clergy back away from any possibility of the supernatural for a variety of reasons. In the past several decades, Catholic seminary training has been character-ized by skepticism, a mindset that dismisses the super-natural or mysterious in the gospel narratives of the life of Our Lord. This is often done in the name of a "scientific point of view," which is really a serious, though popular, misunderstanding of the nature and limitations of natu-ral science. Science, as we define it in common usage, is strictly limited to the tangible and measurable. The only authentic contribution science can make to understand-ing supernatural phenomena is to indicate that they have no known physical explanation. According to Einstein, our "frail and feeble minds" can only perceive in a primi-tive way "the highest wisdom and most radiant beauty . . . which is revealed in the incomprehensible universe."[3] The observable skepticism of much theological and bibli-cal studies leads to a knee-jerk negative reaction, even on the part of those who handle divine mysteries like the Eucharist. Those who are skeptical about the physical res-urrection of Christ will dismiss any account of the Marian appearances at Fatima, even though the best authenticated theophany in human history occurred there. There were tens of thousands of witnesses, and accounts were given in the anti-Catholic secular press of the time.

A theophany is a direct manifestation of the divine presence and power, witnessed by all those present, whether believers or not. The miracle of the sun is an example of a theophany, which occurred at Fatima on October 13, 1917. It should have shaken the whole human race, but we still have ears that do not hear and eyes that do not see.

Another reason for clerical disinterest in approved apparitions like Lourdes and Fatima is that all real or imagined supernatural events quickly become overlaid with exaggerations and dubious details. This happens at times even with sincere witnesses of a miraculous occurrence. A notable exception to this is the shrewd peasant girl Bernadette Soubirous. The remarkable young girl of fourteen would not say that she had seen the Blessed Virgin for a long time. She referred to the person in the grotto simply as "the lady." After repeated requests from Bernadette to reveal her identity, the lady told her, "I am the Immaculate Conception"—a term Bernadette would not have been familiar with and was unlikely to make up. Bernadette never added to her original testimony and consistently refused to approve any artistic representation of what she had seen, even when the artist had carefully followed her own description.

A skilled non-Catholic writer who is professor of religious studies has made a serious attempt to record the original testimony of two approved Marian apparitions (Lourdes and Fatima), two that are consistently challenged (Medjugorje and Garabandal), and two that have been discounted. Sandra Zimdars-Swartz's book, *Encountering Mary*, is a fascinating addition to any priest's library and a useful volume for guiding laity who have a healthy spiritual interest in Marian apparitions.[4]

If we step back a little from any controversy and view modern Church history, it becomes clear that without a series of apparitions and private revelations generally approved by the Church (including the devotions to the Sacred Heart of Jesus and the Divine Mercy), several facts emerge.

First, modern Church history would be considerably different and far less engaging without the revelations of Christ and Mary. With them we are a far richer, stronger, and more engaging Church—something Karl Rahner pointed out in *Sacramentum Mundi*.

Second, no private revelation given to an adult has been generally approved by the Church, and at least implicitly by the Pope, in three hundred years if the identity of the individual was publicly known at the time of his or her death. (This fact can save a lot of discussion with enthusiasts for the latest reports of private revelations.) Examples of adult visionaries unknown at death include Saints Margaret Mary, Catherine Labouré, and Faustina. Youthful visionaries, who naively reveal things, need to be seen differently. Countless reports, some of them quite interesting, have been rejected by the Church simply because they seem to have been derived from the experiences of others and have received a great deal of publicity.

When I hear reports of the latest visionary and the attendant obviously exaggerated claims, warning people that they must do this or that, I tend to flee. When alleged private revelations are accompanied by publicity or even public relations techniques leading to material gain for the person and their supporters, I write them off without further ado. When I follow that course of action, I have yet to make a mistake. I write with the authority of experience in this matter. As the author of *A Still, Small Voice*, I receive at least one private revelation a month, usually rushed urgently by overnight mail. If there has been publicity, the account is sent back immediately to the sender. If God wants a private revelation accepted and a message to be disseminated in his Church, he will, in his providence, see to it. He will overcome all obstacles, changing minds and hearts to accept the truth of his message.

You may therefore ask: Why bother with private revelations at all? That brings us to the third fact that comes to light when we view these matters dispassionately. If a private revelation has been given, it does not have to fit into the plan of human beings. If it is authentic, it comes from God, and the scriptures clearly tell us that he does not consult human beings before he acts. He opens and no one closes; he closes and no one opens (see Is 22:22). An accurate account of Marian apparitions in the past two hundred years makes this obvious. The universally accepted ones, like La Salette, Lourdes, and Fatima, as well as less well-known examples like Pontmain and Beauraing, were all given to ordinary simple souls.[5] A Mexican peasant farmer, shepherds, children of humble parents, an uneducated lay sister, and a contemplative nun were among those so favored by heaven. Thankfully, members of the clergy almost never report supernatural phenomena of their own to the chancery. No doubt they would be sent immediately for residential treatment if they said they had seen Our Lady.

This is nothing new. Local clergy of the time did not react well to the miracles of the Messiah, which should have been convincing. In the gospels we find the same ragtag group following Our Lord and being impressed with his teaching. Their counterparts are the enthusiasts of today—mostly women, many of them very ordinary, and occasionally some people with a degree of prestige. The different responses of various groups to Christ have parallels today. For example, the Knights and Dames of Malta go annually to Lourdes as real pilgrims, helping with the sick for several days at a time. Can you imagine a similar pilgrimage made up of bishops and priests? I cannot.

Are there any general conclusions to be drawn about this mysterious subject? If you are willing to admit that God can admonish and direct us through apparitions, it would be wise at least to be attentive to those that have been approved. Marian apparitions have some general themes: the need for holiness of life, devotion, penance, and prayer, especially the rosary. The John Paul II generation is already champing at the bit to bring all this about after the recent Catholic excursus into iconoclasm and skepticism. It might be helpful to become familiar with the remarkable testimonies to God's miraculous signs, particularly healing. The testimony of Alexis Carrel, for example, Nobel prizewinner in medicine, who actually witnessed a healing take place, is well worth reviewing.[6]

As I look at my own life, I ask myself how in fact I have devotion to the Blessed Mother. It's true that I am fascinated by the authentic accounts of mystical appearances. Like Einstein, I think that the highest expression of the human experience is the "mystical," and that a person who does not look at reality with a sense of wonder and awe might as well be dead.[7] There must, however, be something more personal. For some people, the Blessed Virgin is a spiritual mother figure. For others, she is a protector, while many find in her a cherished intercessor. And indeed, who could be better?

As I was preparing this article, I had to meditate on what the Blessed Virgin meant to me. Her importance has been significant for a very long time, for it was at her shrine in the Church of Our Lady of Victories in Jersey City that, at the age of seven, I came to the realization in an instant that I was supposed to be a priest and not a fireman.

As I analyze my relationship, it seems to be a rather ordinary, unexciting, un-mystical one. The Blessed Mother is the mother of my best Friend. In all the difficulties and burdens of life, I have been able to go on only because I knew that Jesus Christ knew who I was, cared for me, and looked out for me. In my relationships with other people, even difficult people, I remembered that he watched out and cared for them also. Unfortunately, many times I forgot that. Without doubt, he is more present to me than I am to myself, because in times of distraction and anxiety, I almost fail to reflect on who I am. Whenever I stop, he is there. If I am realistic, which I try to be, his Mother is not there. The Blessed Virgin Mary is in eternal glory in heaven. There are a few places on earth where we seem to be able intuitively to pick up her presence, such as the shrine of the Miraculous Medal in the Rue du Bac, in Paris. In that privileged chapel, there is an uncanny sense of her presence. In this world, however, it is Christ who is with us, and through the divine omnipotence and omniscience we invoke the Blessed Virgin and the saints. Somehow or other, in the divine plan she seems to be listening. I don't know how she listens to all the people who pray to her, but I accept the Church's tradition that she is listening to each of us.

My favorite prayer is the one written by the old blind monk, Blessed Herman of Reichenau, who had cerebral palsy and spina bifida. The words of the "Hail, Holy

Queen" sound almost as if they had been written for people who live in New York—"in this valley of tears." This prayer sums it all up, and that is how I talk to my best Friend's mother.

We may well ask how the Blessed Mother helps us. She certainly prays for us, and in my own case I have often asked my best Friend's mother to put in a good word. Anyone familiar with Marian devotion knows that Our Lady may help us in two ways. First, through her intercession we may realize that things did not go as badly as we might have expected them to, or perhaps they even vastly improved (that is rare). The second aspect we experience with this devotion is that we receive the courage to go on. In the film *The Passion of the Christ*, Mary is portrayed as the one who goes on in the worst of circumstances; it is a most powerful image. Many Protestant people are more interested now in Mary than they have been for centuries because of that portrayal. Surely, the Mother of Christ prayed at every step of her Son's passion that "it wouldn't happen," that he wouldn't be scourged, crowned with thorns, made to drag the cross, or crucified. But all those things did happen. What did she do? She remained faithful and believing, and although it is not emphasized in the gospel, she surely had the most incredible and rewarding experience that any human being in great suffering ever had. I cannot help thinking how beneficial it would be if we had some record of the Blessed Virgin's response to the resurrection of Christ. An old Franciscan tradition maintains that Christ appeared to Mary after his resurrection and before the events related in the gospel. Can you imagine any good Jewish boy coming back from the dead and not going to see his mother? This mysterious aspect of Our Lady of Sorrows is often most helpful to me.

Every priest should ask himself whether he tries to follow Our Lady's counsel of prayer and penance, and develop a real love and knowledge of the poor and humble, to whom she regularly appeared. Hands-on work with the poor and needy, accompanied by prayerful meditation, can open a powerful and deeply moving vista in a priest's busy life as he struggles to serve Christ in these unbelieving times. Our Lady has promised her protection to those who devoutly seek it. Real devotion to the Mother of God is like virtue: it is its own reward.

six

Mary: The Perspective of a Parish Priest

Rev. Msgr. Peter J. Vaghi

For a parish priest almost anywhere in the world, it is commonplace to hear the repetitive and lilting sound of the Hail Mary in a parish church before or after daily Mass. Inevitably, there is a faithful group of parishioners reciting aloud decades after decades of the rosary.

This daily devotion is a powerful witness that subtly but surely affects the spiritual life of every parish priest. The sound of this prayer resonates in our priestly hearts, even if we are unable to join in with our parishioners. The rosary is, after all, a powerful and perduring example of the unique and lasting devotion to Mary that rests in the heart of the Church. It is a prayer loved by many priests and laity alike and represents Mary's particular role in our lives, especially those of us privileged to be parish priests. "Simple yet profound, it still remains, at the dawn of this third millennium, a prayer of great significance, destined to bring forth a harvest of holiness."[1]

The rosary has brought joy into my own life as a priest and has deepened my life of prayer. A few summers ago, I was visiting the beautiful Shrine of Our Lady of Pompeii in Italy. On a very hot morning before the tomb of Blessed Bartolo Longo, the nineteenth-century lawyer who did more than anyone to raise the money for that shrine to our Lady of the Rosary, I had a most wonderful experience while praying the Luminous Mysteries. I was given the grace to see in them a kind of road map to lay spirituality as I contemplated the various mysteries of the public life of Christ. I could see their relating uniquely to the different stages in the growth of a lay Christian. Each of us has been graced with our own spiritual insights as we ponder the life of Christ. For me, it was the rosary that led me in that direction. And it continues to do so.

In fact, in his apostolic letter *Rosarium Virginis Mariae*, our late Holy Father John Paul wrote: "To recite the Rosary is nothing other than to contemplate with Mary the face of Christ" (RVM 3). He repeatedly emphasized that although the rosary is clearly Marian in character, it is at its heart a christocentric prayer, an insight that I received at Pompeii, and an insight that is daily with me.

The rosary, with its twenty mysteries, including the new Luminous Mysteries given to us by John Paul II, is a "compendium of the entire gospel," a snapshot of our faith.[2] "It is an echo of the prayer of Mary, her perennial Magnificat for the work of the redemptive incarnation which began in her virginal womb. With the rosary, the Christian people sits at the school of Mary and is led to contemplate the beauty on the face of Christ and to experience the depths of his love" (RVM 1).

You may have had a similar experience when praying the rosary as I have had—a deep sense of consolation, a sense of Mary's maternal presence. It is a witness to her abiding love for us. This seems to happen most when we turn to her in time of particular need.

Mary was there for me in a special way after the death of my mother. So often, the death of one's mother is a particularly challenging time in the life of a priest, as it was for me. I experienced Mary's deep maternal love for me. She is, after all, Mother of Christ, Mother of the Church, and, importantly, Mother of Priests. These are not simply empty titles. They are living realities that have a concrete spiritual effect. This was and continues to be my own experience, an experience of her bountiful love and consolation especially in praying the rosary.

It is as if Our Lady were praying along with me each of the decades of the rosary. Our faith teaches us that Mary intercedes for us as do all the saints. And Mary is Queen of the Saints. She has a place of preeminence among those holy men and women who have gone before us. In each of the mysteries, the Joyful, Sorrowful, Glorious, and now the Luminous Mysteries, her wonderful and powerful presence can be felt.

"If the Liturgy, as the activity of Christ and the Church, is the saving action par excellence, the Rosary too, as a 'meditation' with Mary on Christ, is a salutary contemplation. By immersing us in the mysteries of the Redeemer's life, it ensures that what he has done and what the liturgy makes present is profoundly assimilated and shapes our existence" (RVM 13). In remembering the saving activities that the twenty mysteries represent, in a certain way, they become present in our lives under the guidance of the Holy Spirit and presence of Our Lady. Mary lived with

Jesus. She was his mother. Her eyes were always fixed on him. Her heart was broken because of what happened to him as would be the feeling of any of our own mothers.

She thus has memories of her Son. "In a way those memories were to be the 'rosary' which she recited uninterruptedly throughout her earthly life"(RVM 11), a kind of living rosary. As such, "in the recitation of the rosary, the Christian community enters into contact with the memories and the contemplative gaze of Mary" (RVM 11). Moreover, "the Rosary mystically transports us to Mary's side as she is busy watching over the human growth of Christ in the home of Nazareth. This enables her to train us and to mold us with the same care, until Christ is 'fully formed' in us" (cf. Gal 4:19) (RVM 15). As we grow in our knowledge of the Lord Jesus, we are turned more and more to him in prayer. "If Jesus, the one Mediator, is the Way of our prayer, then Mary, his purest and most transparent reflection, shows us the Way . . . she intercedes for us before the Father who filled her with grace and before the Son born of her womb, praying with and for us" (RVM 16).

And she does this in a joyful spirit. The rosary comes from the word "rose garden," and the rose is a symbol of joy. In that sixteenth century Litany of Loreto, Mary is appropriately referred to as "cause of our joy." So she is as she brought Christ to us. He is the joy of our lives, the joy of our priesthood. Mary, too, in her Magnificat states, "My spirit rejoices in God my Savior" (Lk 1:47). Even as she is the cause of our joy, she is filled with joy herself knowing that the Savior of the world would be born in her womb. The *Regina Caeli*, which we pray during the Easter time, reminds us of the joy of Mary at the resurrection of her

Son, prolonging throughout time the greeting of joy given Mary at the Annunciation.

From Mary and her spirituality, each of us is led to a deeper joy in Christ and in his priesthood. She beautifully models this sense of joy in the five Joyful Mysteries of the rosary to which I now turn. Each of these five mysteries, from the Gospel of Saint Luke, becomes a model for us who share in the priesthood of her Son. The five Joyful Mysteries give us a path to her Son from her spiritual journey, a kind of Marian spirituality for priests.

First Joyful Mystery: The Annunciation

How can we not hear in Mary's obedience of faith, her free consent to be the Mother of the "Son of the Most High," our own priestly promise on the day of our ordination, our promise of obedience and respect to our bishop and his successors, and above all, to the Lord himself? In Mary, and in her free acceptance of the Word of God given by an angel, each of us can also see reflected the trusting yes to God's word of each baptized person. This invitation is offered daily to each of us, all the more as his priest-sons.

And that haunting hymn that we heard on the day of our ordination, and at so many ordination liturgies: "Here I am Lord, I come to do your will!" (cf. Ps 40). Is that not a Marian dimension to our priestly promise of obedience? In her *fiat*, she became a vessel and instrument of God's grace in a totally unique and powerful way. Each priest, by virtue of his office, is also an instrument of God's grace after the example of Mary who bore him in her womb. This example of Marian spirituality from the first Joyful

Mystery is an encouraging model for us who seek to follow his word each and every day by the movement of the Spirit in our daily priestly choices.

Second Joyful Mystery: The Visitation

After Mary's *fiat*, moved by the inner promptings of the Holy Spirit, she traveled to the hill country "in haste" (Lk 1:39). It was the first thing Mary did after the annunciation. There is a sense of urgency in the air as this young girl, our Blessed Mother, hastens with child into the Judean hills, a journey of some 130 miles from Nazareth, to visit her elder cousin, who was also with child in her time of need. At its surface, this is a mission of charity. It is a mission of love. But beneath the surface, the face of Christian charity, the urgency of a response to the Holy Spirit, defines this visitation.

It is almost as if Mary forgot about herself. While she herself was with child, she was filled with charity and love for Elizabeth. Her generosity and the urgency of her response is a powerful model for us priests. How many times are we called to the door of the rectory at a seemingly inopportune time, or are awakened to anoint a dying parishioner in the middle of the night? Mary's response, the urgency and generosity of her spirit, is a guide for us priests. There is an urgency about the celibate love that we promise to live. Urgency, the movement "in haste," is often integral to the priestly love that the spirituality of our Blessed Mother compellingly models. In a homily to new cardinals, Benedict XVI, referring to Mary's movement "in haste," underscores that "The Virgin's initiative was one of genuine charity. . . . Those who love forget about themselves and place themselves at the service of their neighbor. Here we have the image and model of the Church."[3]

On that same occasion of her visitation, Mary recites the Magnificat, which is a part of our evening prayer of the Liturgy of the Hours, which we promise at our ordination to the diaconate to pray. The canticle begins: "My soul proclaims the greatness of the Lord; my spirit rejoices in God my savior" (Lk 1:46–77). In his encyclical letter, *Deus Caritas Est*, Pope Benedict, referring to that opening line of Mary's Magnificat, writes: "In these words she expresses her whole programme of life: not setting herself at the centre, but leaving space for God, who is encountered both in prayer and in the service of neighbor—only then does goodness enter the world" (DCE 41). Could there be a better description of our daily challenge as priests than with Mary to leave "a space for God," especially in our countless acts of charity that define our priestly existence? This second Joyful Mystery helps us see in Mary's visitation the joy that can be ours as priests as we move "in haste" in our daily lives carrying him to whom we are configured.

Third Joyful Mystery: The Nativity

When Jesus took on flesh at Bethlehem, his purpose was to offer his flesh for the life and salvation of the world. He was born in a manger in Bethlehem, a town that providentially means "house of bread." The same Jesus who was laid in a manger is now himself sustenance for the world in the bread of the Eucharist. In this way, the incarnation finds its completion in the Eucharist, the daily Eucharist entrusted to those privileged to be his priests.

From this blessed food of life, each priest draws particular vigor in his mission to live the life of charity and love that the Eucharistic sacrifice represents. As Pope Benedict XVI wrote in *Deus Caritas Est*, "'Worship' itself, Eucharistic communion, includes the reality of being loved and of loving others in turn. A Eucharist which does not pass over into the concrete practice of love is intrinsically fragmented" (DCE 14). This characterization is all the more applicable to the life of a priest!

How can a priest, a parish priest, who offers Mass daily for his people, think of the nativity of the Lord Jesus without meditating on the privilege of himself being configured to Christ the High Priest? He is configured *in persona Christi*, the same Christ born at Bethlehem. When a priest offers Mass, he does so *in persona Christi*. When a priest baptizes or hears confessions, it is really Christ himself who baptizes and hears confessions. Our mission as priests is linked to the child, born of Mary, at Bethlehem.

And that child, in the words of St. Paul: ". . . though he was in the form of God, did not regard equality with God something to be grasped. Rather, he emptied himself, taking the form of a slave, coming in human likeness; and found human in appearance" (Phil 2:6–8). Born of Mary, he was wrapped in swaddling clothes and laid in a manger where animals feed, because there was no room in the inn. He was surrounded by animals and thus understood poverty from the moment of his self-emptying. And all creation rejoiced at the "good news of great joy" (Lk 2:10).

In the Marian spirituality of Bethlehem, we can see ourselves, as priests, linked to the poverty of Jesus and at the same time linked to the wealth of One born of Mary to be the Savior of the world. This poverty is made so often manifest in our detachment from our personal desires. This detachment for the sake of others brings a richness of spirit in the emptying of ourselves in daily service. This is the true poverty of priests in ministry.

Fourth Joyful Mystery: The Presentation

For a parish priest, the church building is an important and essential part of our ministry. It is where, as in the Presentation, sacrifice is offered. It is where each one of us encounters the Lord most fundamentally in the sacrifice of the Mass. It is where parents bring their children each Sunday and where they meet our God and they meet and hear us.

The most profound sacrifice at the altar is foreshadowed in this mystery of the rosary where Mary's firstborn is consecrated to God, and a sacrifice is made on that occasion according to Jewish law. It is also where the trust of Simeon is vindicated that he would not die before he had seen the Messiah.

Oh, how the Holy Spirit, that oft-forgotten Person of the Blessed Trinity, led Simeon and overshadowed him and allowed him to embrace the Lord Jesus and see in Jesus the "light" to the Gentiles for each of us! In the power of the Holy Spirit, each of us is enlightened in our prayerful and daily reading of the divine office and the scriptures that make up the living word of God. The Spirit makes God's holy Word trustworthy and real in our work as priests.

And how we identify with Mary and the prophecy that a sword would pierce her heart! In her joy at bringing the child Jesus into the world, she would also experience his suffering and death. Without the cross, Christianity is anemic. That truth is integral to our faith. So many unique experiences of the parish priest lend themselves to suffering, even as we seek to bring Christ into our world with joy—moments of rejection, misunderstanding, trial, fear, possible disappointment at the change of assignments, and loneliness.

Jesus is the sign of contradiction. Our priesthood reflects, or should reflect, that sublime truth in our own lives. At the same time, Mary, as our ever present consolation and maternal support, lessens the deleterious effect of that truth. The fourth Joyful Mystery leads us to embrace, as Mary embraced, that profound reality in our lives.

Fifth Joyful Mystery: Finding Jesus in the Temple

Jesus was lost. It took a family, his family, to find him. They found him precisely where our people should find us: "sitting in the midst of the teachers, listening to them and asking them questions" (Lk 2:46). Each priest is called to teach, guide, and sanctify. Perhaps we delegate too often that most important role, that essential role of teaching the faith! We are fortunate to possess the new *Catechism of the Catholic Church* and its companion, *The United States Catholic Catechism for Adults*, as excellent and helpful tools in teaching as Jesus taught and continues to teach in and through each of us and the Holy Spirit.

In this last of the Joyful Mysteries, Mary and Joseph also signal the importance of seeking out the lost. In our case as priests, over and over again we are challenged to go after the lost sheep in our care—those marginalized, those alienated from the Church, those lost to God's grace and the beauty of reconciliation.

In many parishes, efforts such as "Come Home for Christmas" campaigns mirror the search of Mary and Joseph for Jesus. They seek the lost sheep, the Jesus in the hearts of those alienated and lost. What a profound joy for a priest to hear the confession of one away from the Church for a long time, or to help resolve a marriage difficulty that has barred a person from the sacramental life! The Church exists to evangelize, and this last of the Joyful Mysteries is a ringing endorsement of that truth. No one can be lost forever from God if we, as priests, together with our lay faithful, seek to find them and bring them home. It is there, in the home of the Church that, like Jesus, each of us advances in "wisdom and age and favor before God and man" (Lk 2:52).

With Mary, as we contemplate each of these five Joyful Mysteries, how can her priests not pray aloud over and over again that canticle of joy: "My soul proclaims the greatness of the Lord; my spirit rejoices in God my savior" (Lk 1:46–47)? There is a joy to priesthood, to the unique priesthood lived out in the many parishes of our world, a joy represented by and in the Joyful Mysteries of the rosary. It is Mary's special prayer and our prayer to treasure each and every day of our priestly lives.

seven

Mary's House

Rev. Msgr. Walter R. Rossi

D uring the course of her almost ninety-year history, the Basilica of the National Shrine of the Immaculate Conception has served as a spiritual oasis for Catholics throughout the United States. With seventy chapels and oratories dedicated to Our Lady, Mary's House is as diverse and multi-cultural as the United States of America. Reflecting the constantly changing face of our nation, each chapel embodies the faith and devotion of immigrant Catholics who claim Mary as their own.

Since the earliest days of Christianity, Our Lady has held a central role in the life of the Church and Christian spirituality. Catholics and non-Catholics venerate Mary as the model to emulate in placing one's life in God's hands and at God's service. Marian devotion has consistently been encouraged by the popes and by the councils of the Church, resulting in the Marian proclamations that are captured in stone in the east and west transepts of the shrine's upper church.

One would be hard-pressed to find an individual who was unfamiliar with the devotion that Pope John Paul II had for Our Lady. His entire priestly, episcopal, and papal ministry was placed in Mary's care. *Totus Tuus* was the motto by which John Paul II lived and ended his life. *Totus Tuus* is an abbreviated form of the entrustment: *Totus tuus ego sum et omnia mea Tua sunt. Accipio Te in mea omnia. Praebe mihi cor Tuum, Maria.* (I belong to you entirely, and all that I possess is yours. I take you into everything that is mine. Give me your heart, O Mary.) During his almost twenty-seven-year pontificate, the Holy Father devoted eighty-six of his Wednesday General Audience catecheses to the virtues and role of the Blessed Virgin Mary. For Pope John Paul II, the Blessed Virgin served as mother, teacher, and guide.

Like his predecessor, Pope Benedict XVI counsels believers to place themselves in the "School of Mary," allowing her to be the guide in learning who Jesus is and becoming conformed to him. With these sentiments, Pope Benedict concluded his address to men and women religious during his 2006 pilgrimage to Poland, encouraging, "If you place yourselves in the school of Mary . . . you will experience for yourselves that God is love and you will transmit this message to the world."[1]

Without question, the Basilica of the National Shrine of the Immaculate Conception has served as a "School of Mary," in which countless pilgrims have encountered God's love and Mary's maternal solicitude. As one moves from chapel to chapel, a wealth of Marian spirituality unfolds. The recitation of rosaries, pilgrims kneeling in prayer as they light a candle or gaze with imploring eyes upon an image of Our Lady, bears witness to their devotion and love.

The dedication of American Catholics and pilgrims throughout the world is most clearly evident when the great upper church is filled for liturgical celebrations. Worshipers make the shrine come to life! Processions with Madonnas from varying nations of the world—ethnic communities seeking to have "their own" chapel honoring the Blessed Mother as she is venerated in their native land—and visitors from every walk of life testify that veneration of Our Lady remains central in the life of the Catholic faithful.

While the devotion of pilgrims at Mary's House is easily recognized during a visit to the shrine or on televised liturgies, the devotion of priests to Our Lady often goes unnoticed. As is normally the case, priests are viewed in their ministerial role as pastors, whose faults are quickly identified and whose virtues are rarely extolled. Outside of the celebration of the Mass and the other sacraments, most people do not see the active prayer life of their priests. They see the administrator, the caretaker, the one who is acting on their behalf before God, but not the man of prayer.

Amid the demands of parish life, it is not always easy for a priest to pray in his parish. To be a man of prayer is the primary obligation of the priest. Pope John Paul II once remarked, "Liturgical and personal prayer, not the tasks of management, must define the rhythms of a priest's life, even in the busiest of parishes."[2] Our Lady's shrine provides an environment in which a priest may exercise this aspect of his life, to "come away . . . and rest a while" (Mk 6:31). It is in this rest, this prayerful respite at Mary's

House, that a priest may be nurtured and his life of devotion sustained as he places himself in the Virgin's care.

Set amid religious houses, the Catholic University of America, and Theological College, Mary's shrine witnesses the unseen devotion of countless priests and seminarians to Our Lady. It is not unusual to walk by the Blessed Sacrament Chapel, a gift of priests from throughout the United States in 1970, or to walk through the crypt church and find priests making a holy hour or praying the rosary or the Liturgy of the Hours. With a schedule allowing ample opportunity to celebrate the Sacrament of Reconciliation, the National Shrine is the beneficiary of priests exercising their ministry as well as being ministered to in this healing sacrament. Because the shrine is located in the heart of so many Catholic institutions, many priests come to the shrine on a regular basis to celebrate Mass. Priests and lay visitors to Mary's House often comment that they like the liturgies at the shrine and find that even within the grand space, there is a peacefulness that pervades Mary's House.

More than ten years ago when I was a parochial vicar in my home Diocese of Scranton, I had the good fortune of being Director of Pilgrimages for the diocese. The primary focus of this position was to lead pilgrimages to the National Shrine in Washington, D.C. This also served as my introduction to "America's Patronal Church." Little did I know then that, one day, I would be assigned to this magnificent Marian sanctuary.

Being at Mary's House has been a great blessing. Priests and lay people often remark that it must be wonderful to be assigned to the shrine. I quickly respond that I am fortunate, because it is in very few assignments that a priest can have the privilege of witnessing the faith of people from all over the world. Young and young at heart, men and women, black, white, Asian, and Latino, people from every walk of life cross the shrine's threshold to seek Our Lady's intercession, to thank her for her patronage, and to draw closer to her Son.

With individual images of Our Lady and particular devotional practices, the Blessed Mother appears as one like the pilgrim and speaks to them in their own language. Although the ritual expressions are many and the languages diverse, the faith behind the devotion is universal. Our people trust Mary and are confident of her assistance. They are convinced that what they cannot accomplish on their own, Mary can achieve for them. This certainty with which our pilgrims entrust themselves to Our Lady stimulates faith. Through them, faith becomes "real" and tangible, not just notional. The faith of our pilgrims brings Mary's House to life and makes this shrine, built of stone, a living temple of God.

Litanies, novenas, prayers, and poetry have been written in honor of Mary. Among the titles given to her are Mother of the Church, Queen of the Apostles, Queen of All Creation, Mother of Divine Hope, and Mother of God. Each of these has a Votive Mass (Masses of the Blessed Virgin Mary), which a priest may celebrate on days that allow a Mass of the Blessed Mother, usually on a Saturday. The introduction to each Mass provides the theological background and a catechetical instruction that is helpful for incorporating the particular virtue of Our Lady, not only into the homily, but also into one's personal life.

Our Lady is also invoked as the Queen of the Clergy and Mother of Priests. Pope John Paul II advocated, "the priest must take Mary into his own home, finding a place for her in his own life, remaining in habitual union with her in his thoughts, feelings, zeal for the kingdom of God and devotion to her."[3] For countless priests, Mary's House is their home. Not only do they concelebrate at daily and Sunday Mass, but perhaps more priests have been ordained in Mary's House than in any Cathedral in the United States. Many of these priests still return to celebrate the anniversary of their ordination to thank God for the gift of their priesthood and to seek Mary's intercession in their ministry. Recently, a priest celebrated his sixtieth anniversary of ordination at the same altar where he was ordained. He remarked that Mary's House has been a part of his priesthood from the beginning, and it is she who has sustained him for over a half century.

Participating in the life of priests is not something foreign to Mary's shrine. In the mid-1940s, the rector sought approval for the establishment of a Marian Federation made up of priests to promote devotion to Our Lady. In 1962, the National Shrine Board of Trustees and the Archbishop of Washington, Patrick O'Boyle, approved the Priests' Union of Prayer. The purpose of the union was to unite the priests of the United States in prayer under the patronage of Mary Immaculate. Monthly Masses were celebrated for the intentions of priests and bishops, and the rosary was prayed, placing those enrolled in the maternal care of the Blessed Virgin Mary.

As a gift to the clergy during the Jubilee Year 2000, the National Shrine sponsored the first organized priest retreat. Priests from throughout the country convened at Mary's House. We were reminded by former Apostolic Nuncio to the United States, Archbishop Gabriel Montalvo, of the need for priests to be "constantly in contact with the holiness of God" and that the time taken for personal prayer would not only benefit the priest, but also his work. Mary's House provides the environment for this contact.

For all Christians, but most especially for the priest, Mary personifies what it means to live "constantly in contact with the holiness of God." Mary is the perfect example of living in total and perfect submission to the will of God, saying yes to God without reservation. The life of the priest requires the same assent. To place oneself at God's service is not always easy. We prefer to do our own will, not God's. We want things our way and in our time. The Blessed Virgin knew that things do not work that way with God. Mary believed that if she trusted in God, if she cooperated and remained faithful to him, God would remain faithful to her. The same is true for us. We need the confidence of Mary. We need her trust and her faith.

Whatever the Blessed Virgin understood of the great things that God had done for her and in her, she did not know what doing God's will would mean. Yet she accepted. Mary's acceptance of God's will was not passive. She actively embraced it: "I am the handmaid of the Lord. May it be done to me according to your word" (Lk 1:38). The Pastoral Letter of the then National Conference of Catholic Bishops, *Behold Your Mother*, observed "as our Lady's *fiat* at the Annunciation was consummated in her total surrender to the Father's will at the foot of the cross, so too through Mary's inspiration and intercession the priest is offered the grace of Christ to give of himself."[4]

The will of God was at the center of Mary's life. As priests, it should also be ours. Like the Blessed Mother, who was the *Theotokos*, the "God bearer" giving life to Jesus, the Life of the World, we priests are meant to be God bearers and "givers of life" through our ministry. This will only happen if, like Mary, the will of God is central to our life. If it is not, priesthood may become a burden, a chore, or a constant struggle, rather than being a source of life.

As we read the scriptures, we do not find many recorded words of Mary. Of those that we do have, each time Mary speaks, she places herself in God's hands and directs others to do the same. Recall her instruction at Cana, when she told the attendants at the wedding, "Do whatever he tells you" (Jn 2:5). Pope John Paul II once commented that "the Virgin Mary was a model of one who looks in faith and hope, and who prompts us to look with faith and hope to the Savior and encourages the Church to carry out the Father's will by doing whatever Christ tells us." Pope Benedict XVI emphasizes this as well in his first Encyclical Letter, *Deus Caritas Est*, in which he writes, "[Mary] knows that she will only contribute to the salvation of the world if, rather than carrying out her own projects, she places herself completely at the disposal of God's initiatives." [5] For priests, our ministry will only be fruitful and our lives complete, if we look with faith and hope to Jesus and follow Mary's command to "do whatever he tells you."

After the wedding at Cana, the next time Mary is encountered in the scriptures is at the foot of the cross. The dialogue, which takes place between Jesus, Mary, and John the beloved disciple, is the foundation for which we refer to Mary as our Mother. Subsequently, the Blessed Virgin Mary has been invoked as the mother given to us by Jesus at the foot of the cross.

The late Archbishop of Boston, Richard Cardinal Cushing, published a series of reflections on Our Lady in which he commented that the relationship of every priest to the Blessed Mother stems from the words Jesus spoke to John, "Behold, your mother" (Jn 19:26). The cardinal stated:

So many affinities and resemblances link Mary and the priest; so many dependencies exist between the priest and Mary; so great is the need of the priest for Mary that no greater school of priestly virtue or storehouse of priestly strength can be imagined than the life and example of Mary. Mary teaches us the ready, unquestioning response to the will of God, which is the beginning and the perfection of all priestly vocation. Mary teaches us the day in, the day out submission to God's plan and purpose, which is the essence of an obedient priestly life. [6]

Long before Cardinal Cushing, Odo of Canterbury (d. 1200) wrote, "One goes to Christ through Mary, as one goes to the Son through the Mother." Saint Louis de Montfort simplified this expression with his often-quoted axiom, "To Jesus through Mary." Saint Jose Maria Escriva adapted the words of Louis de Montfort, counseling, "To Jesus we always go, and to him we always return, through Mary."[7] With these considerations, the *Catechism of the Catholic Church* teaches that from ancient times, the Blessed Virgin has been honored with the title "Mother of God," to whose protection the faithful fly in all their dangers and needs.[8] Echoing these sentiments, Pope Benedict XVI stated in his homily on the Solemnity of the Assumption of the Blessed Virgin Mary, that she "always listens to us, she is always close to us and being Mother of the Son, participates in the power of the Son and in his goodness. We can always entrust the whole of our lives to this Mother, who is not far from any one of us."[9]

In her wisdom, the Church assists in the sanctification of the life of the Church and of the priest, by the promise made at diaconate ordination to pray the Liturgy of the Hours. In the course of this daily prayer, the priest "flies" to the protection of the Mother of God as he prays the Magnificat at Evening Prayer and a Marian Antiphon at the close of Night Prayer. While the "Hail, Holy Queen" may be the most familiar of the antiphons, the *Alma Redemptoris Mater* remains my favorite, as the hymn recognizes our fallen nature and implores Our Lady's assistance along the path to holiness.

The rosary should also be a part of the priest's daily prayer. Blessed John XXIII listed praying five decades of the rosary each day among the "Little Rules" for the spiritual life he established for himself as a seminarian. As pope, John XXIII extolled the practice of praying the rosary as a "devout form of union with God" and an "uplifting effect on the soul."[10] In days past, the rosary was part of the daily prayer regimen for priests and religious. This should also be the case today. I consider the rosary part of my daily conversation with Mary, through which she forms me in her faith and leads me closer to her son, Jesus.

Pope John Paul II declares in his Apostolic Letter on the Rosary, "to recite the Rosary is nothing other than to contemplate with Mary the face of Christ" and enables us "to be conformed ever more closely to Christ."[11] To be conformed to Christ is the goal of all Christians, but especially of priests. In the rosary, Mary directs us in the ways of her Son and helps us see him more clearly.

For almost nine decades, the Basilica of the National Shrine of the Immaculate Conception has served the Church in the United States as a pilgrimage destination where priests and the lay faithful are able to "contemplate with Mary the face of Christ." The many Marian chapels and oratories in the shrine facilitate such contemplation. One cannot help but "contemplate the face of Christ," as the mosaic of the Christ in Majesty is visible from every corner of the Upper Church.

This contemplation, however, requires that one go beyond image gazing. True Marian spirituality calls for an openness to the activity of the Holy Spirit in our lives and for allowing ourselves to be guided by the Holy Spirit as Mary did. Moreover, the initial call to priesthood stems from an openness to the Holy Spirit and is brought to completion through cooperation with the Holy Spirit. Our priesthood, however, is never complete. Like married couples who live out their sacrament of Marriage each day, so too, the priest must live out his sacrament of Holy Orders each day. By cooperating with the Holy Spirit as Mary did, the priest daily perfects his priesthood.

As I approach Mary's shrine each day, I am continually awed by the grandeur of the building. For me, though, Mary's House is more than a beautiful church. It is a visible reminder that like Mary, I am God's servant, called to do what God asks, and in order to do so, like Mary, I must daily place myself at God's disposal.

Priests, as God's servants, find fulfillment and happiness in their priesthood through the exercise of different ministries. I have found that Mary provides the key to a fruitful priesthood. By uttering her *fiat* at the start of each day, by turning to her for strength and protection as we would to our own mother, by placing ourselves each day in God's hands as did Mary, our souls and our lives will also proclaim "the greatness of the Lord" (Lk 1:46).

eight

Mary and the Divine Presence: A Biblical Reflection

Most Rev. Arthur J. Serratelli

Among the most ancient and important catacombs in Rome are the catacombs of St. Priscilla on the Via Salaria. Painted on the walls of these catacombs are numerous frescos that throw light on the faith of the early Church. One fresco depicts the Virgin Mary seated, with the infant Jesus at her breast. Next to her stands a man pointing to a star directly above. The star was the symbol in Jewish tradition for the Messiah (cf. Num 24:17). Thus, this fresco expresses the mystery of the incarnation: God's Son, the long-awaited Messiah, is born of the Virgin Mary.

Dating from the early 200s, this is the oldest representation in art of Mary and Child. The fresco evidences that, from the very beginning, the Church has placed Mary in a place of honor and devotion. She is the one who is chosen to bring forth the Savior.

Growing up in an Italian parish, I was surrounded by images of Mary. The many titles under which Mary is honored instilled in me even at an early age, the great role God gives Mary in the life of the Church because of her divine maternity. Images are important. They touch our senses. They move our hearts. From the young mother holding the child in the *praesepio*, to the heart-pierced Lady of Sorrows, I learned how much a part of our life the Mother of Jesus remains.

From all eternity, God chose Mary. As Saint Augustine says: "Before the Word was born of the Virgin, he had already predestined her as his mother" (*Iohannis Evangelium Tractatus* VIII, 9). But God respects the creature he made. He leaves her free. In freely cooperating with God, Mary becomes the model for all disciples.

During his public life, Jesus holds up Mary as the model of what true discipleship means. In the only scene where Mary appears in the tradition common to all the synoptic Gospels, a group of disciples is seated around Jesus in the house of Simon Peter. Jesus' family comes looking for him. Once Jesus is told that his mother and family are outside, he points to those on the inside and says, "Here are my mother and my brothers. (For) whoever does the will of God is my brother and sister and mother" (Mk 3:34–35). Jesus defines family not on the basis of blood, but on attachment to the will of God.[1] Nazareth is giving way to Capernaum.

Certainly the early followers of Jesus found strength in his words. In so many cases they had to break the bonds of family. Following Jesus always implies a choice. He must come first. His proclamation of the kingdom takes precedence over any other priority. In Old Testament times, Elisha consents to be a disciple of Elijah, but only on the condition that he returns home to take leave of his family. Elijah agrees (cf. 1 Kg 19:20–21). Not so with Jesus. He warns his would-be followers that they are not permitted to put any condition on their discipleship. He demands total and unreserved loyalty. Reversing the decision of Elijah, Jesus says, "No one who sets a hand to the plow and looks to what was left behind is fit for the kingdom of God" (Lk 9:62). To the would-be disciple who wants to stay at home until his father dies and all family obligations are fulfilled, Jesus swiftly replies, "Follow me, and let the dead bury their dead" (Mt 8:22).

The eschatological family replaces the physical family, but it does not reject it. Luke certainly understands this. He portrays Mary as one of those who truly hears God's word and keeps it (cf. Lk 8:19–21).[2] As priests, the demands of our ministry and the duty to our family call for time and commitment. Sharing in the apostolic ministry of Jesus helps us deepen, not destroy, the natural bonds of human affection. Did not Mary remain with Jesus from Cana to Calvary? How many of us have had the joy of our mothers and fathers, so filled with faith, support us in our priesthood, joining their prayer to our efforts! Being loved by our own, it becomes easier to love others.

When the angel Gabriel appears to Zechariah and sets in motion the events immediately surrounding the coming of the Messiah, the angel appears to him where angels are expected to be. "Then an angel of the Lord appeared to him, standing at the right of the altar of incense"(Lk 1:11). No surprise to find an angel in the Temple in the midst of liturgy. Angels surround the divine presence with their constant praise (cf. Is 6:1–3). But far from the Holy City of Jerusalem, in a town never once mentioned in the Old Testament, the angel Gabriel is sent to Mary. "In the sixth month, the angel Gabriel was sent from God to a town in Galilee called Nazareth" (Lk 1:26).

The angel appears to Zechariah, but he is *sent* to Mary. As if an ambassador to a foreign land, the angel comes. The exact place where he meets Mary in Nazareth is left unsaid. From unexpected places, we are called by God. Some of us are called from the innocence of youth; others, from a work already begun. In our priestly vocation, God may use others to be a Gabriel to us to let us know his will. I had the gift of a great pastor who simply invited me to serve Mass daily and led me by example. We need not be afraid to suggest to young men the priestly vocation. And our example does have an effect.

Under the old dispensation, the faithful went up to Jerusalem to meet God. With the sublime mystery of the incarnation, God comes to meet us where we are. The lesson is clear. Every place is sacred. Every place can become a place of encounter between God and his people.[3] It is sometimes difficult to remember that, as priests, we are chosen to bring God wherever we go. In the moments of our sacramental ministry, this truth of our ordination is obvious. But even in the seemingly endless hours of meetings and planning, and in the off hours of relaxation, we need to cultivate an awareness of the grace given us to make God present. I remember the afternoon I was treading up the Janiculum hill in Rome, and a woman wrinkled with age took my hands and kissed them. I had been ordained just that morning. But, from that moment, I knew I had to be more than I was.

At the Annunciation, Gabriel reveals to Mary God's plan that she is to become the mother of Christ. He announces to Mary three truths about the Son she is asked to bear. First, he is the Son of David, the long-awaited

Messiah. Second, he is the Son of God. Third, the Holy Spirit is present with him. This is the same threefold revelation about Jesus made at his baptism (cf. Lk 3:21–22) and preached after Pentecost (cf. Acts 14–36; Rom 1:3–4). It is the *kerygma* of the post-paschal community. And it is found for the first time on the lips of Gabriel. Mary, who hears that word and accepts it, is the first disciple. In the soul of Mary, the faith of the Church is born. She is the first to believe the gospel.[4]

Between Gabriel's announcement and Mary's *fiat*, the whole world trembles in expectation. Mary is the creature in dialogue with the Creator. He waits for her to say yes to his will. Mary questions, "How can this be, since I have no relations with a man?" (Lk 1:34). Abraham asks God how Sarah is to give birth to Isaac since they are both advanced in age (cf. Gen 17:17). Moses questions God about his choice as deliverer (cf. Ex 3:11). And, the prophets Isaiah, Jeremiah, and Ezekiel ask God about their own suitability to carry out his work. Questioning is an exercise of human freedom.

After ordination we approach our first assignment with eagerness. We have freely embraced our call. We are ready to work. But, the day comes when we are very happy in our ministry, and the bishop requests us to take on another assignment. It could be another parish, the role of pastor, special work, or even further studies. We question his wisdom. We doubt our ability. Our freedom opens us to honest dialogue with our bishop. Our obedience helps us to be bold and trusting in accepting what we are asked to do.

Mary's question to Gabriel allows the angel to unfold with greater density the mystery she is called to share. She is now told that the Holy Spirit will come upon her, and the power of the Most High will overshadow her; therefore, her child will be called Son of God (cf. Lk 1:35). These words carry within them the revelation of the child's identity that goes beyond his role as Messiah. Something new is added about Jesus. Something new is said about Mary.

In the Old Testament, the entire nation of Israel is God's son. And the king embodies the nation. On the day the new king ascends the throne, he is adopted as God's son (cf. Ps 2 and Ps 110). The prophet Nathan had promised David that God would raise up the Messiah from among his descendants (cf. 2 Sam 7). Gabriel's words to Mary echo this prophecy. This child of Mary is the long-awaited Messiah. But Mary's child is God's Son as no other person ever was in the history of Israel. Gabriel's words contain this deep mystery of the divinity of Jesus.

The angel's greeting to Mary already hints at this. Gabriel addresses Mary with the words, "The Lord is with you" (Lk 1:28). This greeting is freighted with meaning. But, in light of the identity of Mary's child, these words take on special meaning.

In the Old Testament, the presence of God is promised to individuals who are chosen to play a significant role in salvation history. To Isaac who offers no resistance to the Philistines, God says at Beersheba, "I am the God of your father Abraham. You have no need to fear, since *I am with you*. I will bless you" (Gen 26:24). To Jacob, fleeing the land promised Abraham and Isaac, God says at Bethel, "Know that *I am with you*. I will protect you wherever you go, and will bring you back to this land" (Gen 28:15). To Moses, Gideon, and Jeremiah, God makes the same promise.

In each case, the promise of God's presence is given when the destiny of the nation is at stake. God personally assumes responsibility for the events to unfold. The human person is his chosen instrument.[5] No stronger ground can be found for hope. No wonder Mary has nothing to fear. God is with her. He is strength in her weakness, richness in her poverty.

The gift of the Holy Spirit given us through the imposition of hands is God's permanent promise to be with us in our priestly work. We are limited. We are frail. Yet, we have been chosen. So often I discover this grace in the casual remarks people make. "Father, your homily today was exactly what I needed to hear." And the remark comes after a preparation and delivery I thought woefully lacking. God is faithful. God is present. He works through us.

Gabriel explains God's presence to Mary with the image of the overshadowing of the Holy Spirit. In the Old Testament, after Moses builds the sanctuary, the cloud covers the Tent of Meeting, and the glory of God fills the place (cf. Ex 40:35). God is now present. In the desert wandering, the cloud overshadows the Tent of the Testimony. The people know that, as long as the cloud hovers over it, God is there (cf. Num 9:18–22). When the Ark of the Covenant is transferred to the Temple in Jerusalem, the cloud overshadows the place, and the people recognize the presence of God (cf. 2 Chr 5:14). Now the Holy Spirit overshadows Mary. God is present and active. He is truly within Mary. The oft-repeated greeting, "The Lord is with you," takes on fresh meaning. God is tabernacled within Mary.[6]

The mere announcement of the extraordinary intervention of the Holy Spirit fills Mary's soul with awe and wonder. She responds to the angel, "May it be done to me according to your word" (Lk 1:38). Her words anticipate those of her Son, who accepts every detail of his life as coming from the hands of the Father: "My Father . . . your will be done" (Mt 26:42); however, at the Annunciation,

Mary's words have none of the sorrow or pain of Jesus' words in Gethsemane (cf. Lk 22:44). Luke frames Mary's response with the Greek γενοιτο. Her *fiat* is not one of res- ignation or simple acquiescence. Luke uses the optative, for Mary's *fiat* is brimming over with the joy of divine elec- tion. This is Mary's last word to Gabriel. It is the antiphon to the angel's first word of joy to Mary, χηαιρε, "Rejoice" (Lk 1:28).[7] She voices the joy-filled Amen to God's plan that human history has been awaiting since the sin of Adam and Eve.

As a seminary priest for thirty-one years, I helped young men discover God's plan for them. I gently accompanied them to their final yes to God. It was always a moment of great joy. In preparing couples for marriage and leading them beyond the happy and hectic events of the wedding day to a deeper understanding of their conjugal vows, I experienced joy as well. Whenever we strive to open oth- ers to give themselves to God's will, there is joy for them and for us as priests.

Mary's yes allows God to realize in her the great- est vocation a woman was ever asked to live. The Spirit descends on her and she conceives her child, God's only- begotten Son. As the Council of Ephesus defined in 431 AD, Mary is *theotokos*, the Mother of God. And, in her role as the Mother of the Lord, she becomes the model and the mother of all vocations.

Mary images the vocation of every creature. Each of us has been chosen by God. He has willed us into life with a purpose and a mission. He makes his choice in the mystery of his all-loving and eternal providence. And his choice for us goes beyond what we could ever imagine. It often happens to priests that when we respond to a new mission given us by our bishop, we are startled by God's grace. After settling into a very happy ministry of teaching Sacred Scripture, I was given the added work of being rector of our college seminary. This was something I never even thought of. Very quickly, my bishop's words to me became reality. "You will see gifts God has given you that you do not yet realize." Only in time, does God's choice become clear. So it was for Mary, so also for us.

We are called to embrace God's will freely and to live out the vocation he has placed within our heart. Just as Mary's yes to God's plan allows God to accomplish great things, our yes to God allows him to continue his work in us. As Mary's *fiat* is a blessing to Mary and others, so our yes becomes a source of blessing.

Already from the moment of the incarnation, where Mary goes, Jesus goes. In the streets of Nazareth, in the home, in the crowded markets of Jerusalem, there is the Son of God. In the vocation of Mary as bearer of the saving presence of God is our vocation as Christian and, most especially, as priest. Sometimes life seems without glory—monotonous. The daily round of common duties without much glamour. Yet, all the while, we bear to others the saving gift of Jesus.

At the Annunciation, it is enough for Mary to understand that God's plan to save his people will unfold through her son. The angel's message of her virginal conception implicitly reveals the divine sonship of Jesus. But, Mary does not yet understand his full identity, nor is she told of the cross and the resurrection. Receiving the gospel that is Jesus Christ, Mary becomes the depository of a mystery. With complete trust, she begins her unique vocation. Her faith is the flowering of the faith of the entire Old Testament. Slowly and with events yet to happen, Mary's faith will deepen and come to touch the mystery of her son's divine identity and redemptive mission.

Mary at the Annunciation images the Church at Easter. In fact, the Church is Marian before all else. She is called to receive and embrace the Word in faith.[8] With the angel's *paeconium paschale*, the Church becomes the depository of the mystery of redemption. Like Mary, the Church comes to understand that mystery only slowly through the events of history.

This image of the Church as Marian reminds us that discipleship comes before apostleship. As priests, our following of Jesus precedes any mission we receive from the Lord. We need our prayer, our time alone as disciples at the feet of the Master, more than the hours we spend in planning! The image of the Church as Marian rightly challenges us to live the Word before we preach the Word. Furthermore, this image underscores the vocation to priesthood as a gift. Our call to priesthood is given as a grace. Like Mary, we are called to embrace it in total freedom. And, as we live the mystery of our priesthood, we, like her, gradually come to appreciate with greater intensity the grace we are given to bear God's presence in Christ to our world today.

nine

She Will Crush His Head

Rev. Msgr. Stephen J. Rossetti

For a number of years, I have ministered to priests and religious suffering from psychological and spiritual problems. Sometimes their problems are more psychologically based, such as a major depression or a bipolar illness. Other times, their difficulties, while having important psychological bases to them, also carry moral and spiritual overtones, such as various kinds of sexual behaviors.

As a clinician, I am aware of the psychological aspects of these problems. For the good of the client, it is important that I attend to these dynamics. But as a priest, I also am acutely aware of the spiritual dimension. Is there any better way to destroy the vocation and efficacy of a priest than to have his life consumed with a cocaine addiction, alcoholism, internet pornography and/or a long series of sexual contacts? And I would add that I think there is no better way to cripple the work of the Church than to cripple those who minister in her name—her priests and religious.

More than a few educated people do not believe in the existence of a spiritual being that has turned to evil, i.e., Satan. But he is "hell bent" on destroying the Church. Similarly, many do not believe in the existence of a hell in the next life. Or if they do believe, they cannot imagine anyone being there; however, given my years of working with people in difficulty, I readily can. I have seen more than a few people whose lives had already become a *living hell*.

To describe this living hell, I would include the pervasive presence of an inner rage that consumes them. Furthermore, they become mistrustful, isolated, and in a great deal of inner pain. They begin to despair of themselves and cannot imagine a God who loves them personally. Eventually, this self-despair and despairing of God's personal offer of salvation to them can turn into a rage directly aimed at God. As this hell begins to take over their lives, they may become self-destructive in a variety of different ways, such as drugs, alcohol, sex, or suicidal behaviors.

I am *not* suggesting that *all* psychological problems, no matter how destructive, are subjectively sinful and lead one to hell. Indeed, patient endurance of psychological disorders can be a source of sanctification and holiness for many who must endure such trials. But I am convinced that it would be a mistake to draw a clean line between human psychological destruction and a person's spiritual destruction. Just as the presence of true joy and peace in our lives can prefigure the blessedness of heaven, so too can an inner rage and self-destructive behavior prefigure the darkness of hell.

Years ago I recall ministering to a priest who had sexually molested a number of children. In the course of spiritual and psychological treatment, he came to his senses and kind of "woke up," not unlike the prodigal son. He looked at me and said, "You know, my life had been caught up in some real *ontological* evil." By ontological, this priest meant that his life had been assumed into real, objective evil. He believed that he had been lost. The priest repented of his ways, and I had much hope for his future in this life and the next.

Similarly, a number of years ago I was sitting down with another priest and his bishop. The priest had all of the aforementioned horrible symptoms and more. His spiritual life was non-existent, and he was acting out in ways that were grossly contrary to the Christian life and to his vocation. And he was getting worse. Yet he did not seem to grasp the seriousness of his plight. He expressed no intention of changing his life. Finally, I looked at him and said, "You're going down the wrong path." He knew what I meant. So did his bishop.

Satan is an enraged being. He is consumed with a pervasive inner rage; it is perpetually eating him up from the inside. He is like the Gerasene demoniac in scripture who, day and night, screams and gashes himself with stones. This is the lot of those immersed in evil. Never resting, those engulfed in evil are tortured within and are filled with an inner violence. Satan spews forth this violent rage on those around him and on the world. Applying a medieval term, one could say he is *mad*.

Unfortunately, one can see the footprints of this evil throughout the world. I admit that there is much good all around us and we need only open our eyes to see the beauty and the grace, but there is also much violence and evil. It would be foolish to miss it.

The battleground of the spirit is very real in all Christians: "The spirit is willing, but the flesh is weak" (Mt 26:41). But I believe that the spiritual battle is particularly important and waged with a special intensity in our priests. They are configured to Christ in a most unique way, and they are directly engaged in Jesus' mission and ministry.

We might see the three temptations of Jesus in the desert as being three of the primary temptations of priests. We are tempted to *materialism* (turning stones into bread); we are tempted to seek *power and glory* (ruling over kingdoms); and we are tempted to act with *pride and arrogance* (putting God to the test) (cf. Lk 4:1–13).

How are we to fight these temptations? First, I would not overlook the common "weapons" that we all have at hand, such as living a balanced life and using the ordinary means to take care of one's psychological and physical health. It can be surprising how a failure to take care of our bodies and psyches can lead to spiritual problems. For example, a priest recently telephoned me anonymously and told me that his life was spinning out of control. He revealed that he had been working constantly; he had no friends or social life. He was tired, lonely, and isolated. He found that he was facing some very powerful sexual temptations and was losing ground. We talked about how to get his life back in balance and some of the actions he quickly needed to take.

In addition to several sound psychological and physical steps, there are spiritual ones as well. I would definitely add the importance of a strong spiritual life that would typically include, but not be limited to, frequent reception of the sacraments, especially Eucharist and confession, regular prayer, including meditating on scripture, plus praying the Liturgy of the Hours. He will also want to engage a spiritual director to help him get back on track.

But there is one more important part of a healthy spiritual life for a priest, particularly a priest under siege of strong temptations.

The Woman Strikes at His Head

In the book of Genesis, after the sin of Adam and Eve, God said to the serpent, "I will put enmity between you and the woman. . . . He will strike at your head, while you strike at his heel" (3:15). From a theological perspective, this passage has been interpreted to be a prediction of the unending strife between Satan and human beings. This truth is echoed in Vatican II's *Gaudium et Spes*: "For a monumental struggle against the powers of darkness pervades the whole history of man. The battle was joined from the very origins of the world and will continue until the last day, as the Lord has attested" (GS 37). In his encyclical letter *Redemptoris Mater*, John Paul II cited this passage from *Gaudium et Spes* and added: "For Mary, present in the Church as the Mother of the Redeemer, takes part, as a mother, in that monumental struggle" (RM 24).

Moreover, Genesis implies the eventual victory over evil as the descendants of Adam strike at the serpent's head with their heels. While the passage most properly looks to the eventual and definitive victory of Christ, we can find in our Catholic tradition a reference to the Virgin Mary. She is sometimes depicted as the one who strikes at the serpent's head and, invoking the power of her Son, casts out evil. This traditional interpretation of Genesis 3:15 is reiterated in *Ineffabilis Deus,* the Papal Apostolic Constitution that defined the Immaculate Conception: "The most holy Virgin, united with [Jesus] by a most intimate and indissoluble bond, was, with him and through him, eternally at enmity with the evil serpent, and most completely triumphed over him, and thus crushed his head with her immaculate foot."[1]

Similarly, the Book of Revelations speaks of "a woman clothed with the sun, with the moon under her feet, and on her head a crown of twelve stars" (Rev 12:1) whom the dragon, or Satan, tried unsuccessfully to destroy. Then Michael the Archangel and his angels engaged in a battle with the dragon. This image of the woman clothed with the sun appears on Juan Diego's *tilma* at the shrine of Our Lady of Guadalupe in Mexico City.

It is no accident that prayers for casting out evil, including those in Church exorcisms, often mention the Virgin Mary and Michael the Archangel, and invoke Mary's intercession with her Divine Son. The former priest-exorcist of Rome wrote, "The power of the Rosary and devotion to the Virgin Mary [in casting out evil] are well documented."[2]

The theology of the Church is clear: it is the person of Jesus who has cast out the devil; he alone has conquered sin and death. But the Church's theology is rich in the inter-connectedness of all. We are supported and aided by the communion of saints, including our loved ones and those holy men and women who have become part of the Church in the next life. We are aided by that unseen army of angels and saints with whom we are united, even now, in the Body of Christ. Can there be any person more efficacious or closer to Jesus than his Mother, she who was born without the inherent flaws of sin, who gave birth to and raised Jesus, and was first among all his followers? As in *Lumen Gentium*, "Because of this gift of sublime grace she far surpasses all other creatures, both in heaven and on earth" (LG 53).

We Cannot Face Addiction and Evil Alone

With regard to facing temptation and evil, our unbroken tradition is consistent: *Don't do it alone.* In fact, we frail human beings are no match for a direct confrontation with evil. We will lose and lose quickly. Perhaps this offends our self-image. But we must remember it is Christ alone, the God-man, who has conquered evil. It is through our invoking his name, and the intercession of those close to him, such as the Virgin Mary, in which we conquer. The monk and writer Thomas Merton, in a conference with Trappist novices at Gethsemani, said, "[If] the devil is attacking you . . . how are you going to handle his attack? . . . Anything but trusting in your own strength. If you trust in your own strength, you're sunk."[3]

In an analogous way, I see this often with priests in difficulty. Perhaps the greatest challenge in the entire process of healing is their willingness to admit they have a problem and to ask someone else for help. We priests can be a very independent lot. This is not entirely a bad thing because our ministerial lives usually require that we be self-starters. Each day, we must discern what needs to be done and do it; however, when we have personal problems, we are usually our own worst enemies.

Whether we are battling an addiction to alcohol or battling demonic temptations, we cannot rely solely on our own strength. We must look quickly and confidently to others for aid. Whether we use the instruments of a therapist or Twelve Step groups for healing from addiction, or look to the heavens for help in overcoming the lure of sin and evil, it is critical that we have the humility to realize that we cannot do it alone. I have little hope for the isolated priest who cannot ask for help.

On January 23, 1840, parishioners in Ars, France, overheard a conversation between the saintly Curé of Ars, the patron of parish priests, and a woman who was possessed. They heard a voice coming from the possessed woman say to St. John Vianney, "Without that [here he used a word of repulsive coarseness to designate our Lady] who is up above, we should have thee for certain; but she protects thee, together with that great dragon [St. Michael], who is at the door of thy church."[4]

And if we think such days of priests battling evil are over, I recently heard from a priest who had a similar encounter. He relayed that it was late at night in his room. He was suddenly and quickly spiritually attacked by demonic forces. While nothing could be seen, he made it very clear that there was no doubt in his mind what was taking place. He indicated that he realized he would be quickly overcome by this evil presence and that he was certainly no match for such unbelievable power. He knew that he needed help and he said that he barely made it to the other side of the room where his rosary beads lay. The moment he grasped the beads, the demonic force left.

The priest mentioned that, since that time, his rosary beads are never far from his side. This experience carries clear signs of authenticity and is theologically sound, which argues in favor of its reality. Moreover, the priest's veracity and mental state are not in question. While most of us will not face evil in such explicit and conscious ways, as did the Curé of Ars or the priest above, our battle with evil is no less urgent or real. And our need for the saving power of Christ, through the intercession of Mary and the sword of St. Michael, is no less acute.

It is important for us priests, who are so accustomed to helping others, to have the humility to ask for and to let ourselves receive help from others. A confessor and spiritual director are important guides along the spiritual path. At times, a professional counselor or therapist may be needed when a difficult personal problem surfaces. And we perpetually and universally depend upon the maternal protection of Our Lady and St. Michael in our unseen struggle to walk in the way of goodness.

Our Battle for Integrity

It is not popular today to speak of the great good and tremendous spiritual power given to priests. Nevertheless, as we, ordained priests, minister in the name of Jesus and are instruments of his saving power, we are given great power to do good. We saw what a single humble priest can do in the small, remote town of Ars, France. Jean-Marie Vianney was an instrument of great good because of the holiness of his priestly life. He is a wonderful model, particularly for all of us who engage in priestly ministry.

But this immense power for good can also be turned to great evil. All of us know people who have had their lives changed for the good through the ministry of a priest. But we all know people who have been greatly harmed as well. There are more than a few examples of each. Perhaps there is a little of both in all of our frail priestly lives. It is of particular importance that we recognize the great power of the priesthood and rededicate ourselves to living lives of integrity, and to minimize any damage our personal weaknesses can cause.

I believe it was not incidental to our priesthood that one of the final acts of Jesus before his death was to look at his beloved disciple standing next to his mother and say, "Behold, your mother" (Jn 19:27). Jesus poured out his life for us. He gave us everything he had, including his own mother. While this act is rightly interpreted to symbolize the gift of Mary to all the faithful, it has special meaning and significance for priests. Should we shun such a wonderful gift? Mary will *not* disappoint any of us, particularly her priest-sons.

Mary has a special place in resisting temptation and evil, whether it is in the Rite of Exorcism or more commonly in our daily lives. In a related way, I believe that the ever-virgin Mother of God also has a special place in assisting us to live a chaste and celibate life. She is certainly an image and an encouragement for all of us who strive to live our lives with integrity. This is why I often recommend to priests in the confessional who are struggling, especially with the virtue of chastity, to commend themselves to the Mother of God. These expressed needs of her priest-sons will not go unanswered.

As noted in Vatican II's *Lumen Gentium*, "Yet the followers of Christ still strive to increase in holiness by conquering sin. And so they raise their eyes to Mary who shines forth to the whole community of the elect as a model of the virtues" (LG 65).

Consoling Mother

Since the age of twelve, I have happily worn the Miraculous Medal of Our Lady. I understand that there are a number of promises made to those who wear it with faith. I am not concerned with such promises; I trust that the Lord will bestow his blessings and graces where he sees fit. Rather, I wear it as a reminder and a sign of my connection to the Mother of Jesus. There is no question in my mind that I owe my vocation to the priesthood to the intercession of Mary, and that I serve God in imitation of Christ under her protection. I echo the motto of the great John Paul II, "*Totus tuus.*"

Most of all, I find her presence in my life to be a constant consolation. Gazing upon the loveliness of her radiantly holy face brings me much sweetness and peace of soul. Rather than having a deleterious effect on my faith in Jesus, I find this devotion strengthens my relationship to him. As Von Balthasar wrote, "The veneration of Mary is the surest and shortest way to get close to Christ in a concrete way."[5]

One could certainly go through a priestly life and not have a devotion to the Mother of God. In fact, more than a few good priests apparently do not have such a devotion. Moreover, one could be a very good Christian and not have a devotion to her. We all know some fine Christians who do not. But such a road would be more barren than necessary, more stark than intended by our Savior. And would such a life be in complete and total conformity with the wishes of our Lord?

Jesus poured out his life for us and gave us everything he had, including his mother. The reflective reader of the scriptures would be led to conclude that Mary was an abiding consolation for her Son. She was the first of his disciples in faith. She encouraged others to follow her Son: "Do whatever he tells you" (Jn 2:5). Most importantly, she remained with him at the foot of the cross after others had abandoned him. The Father provided this wonderful gift to the Son. And now this consoling gift is offered to us.

The life of a priest is not an easy one. Jesus promised that the "cup" he drank of, we would drink. Down through the ages, in varying forms and disguises, we have seen a particularly virulent hostility toward the faith and those who stand for it. Our day is no different. Jesus assures us that we will end up on the cross as he did. I find it a consolation to know that Mary will remain with me, too, in these dark times. When she looks at us, she sees men who are configured to her Son, and thus she looks at us with a special tenderness and holy warmth. How could she not love us with a particular love when she sees the face of Christ in us?

When attacked by the evil force from without, or our own weakness from within, we need help. To be a Christian is, by definition, not to go it alone. We are members of a faith community united and filled by the Spirit. Thus, we are given many sources of strength and consolation.

We are given the sacraments that nourish us with the life of Jesus. We are supported by fellow Christians in this world and by the invisible body of saints. And we raise our eyes to Mary. She has a special love for her priest-sons as we do for her. This is one of the great joys of being a priest. For this wonderful grace, I thank God. And I particularly thank Jesus on the cross. His command to us, his parting gift to us, his last words to us should sink deeply into our hearts and bring us great joy: "Behold, your mother."

ten

Mary, Catholicism, and Priesthood

Rev. Gerald O'Collins, S.J.

Many Catholics and other Christians point to visual images and hymns when asked how and why they cherish the Blessed Virgin Mary. Statues, paintings, mosaics, Eastern icons, prayers, poems, and sacred music put into focus their devotion to her. That is certainly true of myself, both as a Catholic and a priest. My love for Mary prompts me to do many things in my priestly ministry, like celebrating her Mass on Saturday, praying the rosary with those in distress, and encouraging those I visit to have an image of her in their homes. We priests and all the families we serve need, more than ever, her presence and blessing.

Beyond question, there is more to say. But let me begin with images, prayers, poetry, and music.

Images of the Virgin Mary

Catholic Christianity exhibits a widespread desire to have a crucifix, not simply a bare cross, displayed in churches. Certainly, an empty cross can emphatically recall Christ's rising into glory; he is no longer personally pinned to that terrifying instrument of suffering and death. All the same, Catholics want to see his body and its wounds. This instinct has also prompted them into erecting, in different parts of the world, wayside scenes of Calvary. At the foot of the cross, Christ's mother keeps her lonely vigil. Many people instinctively feel a deep emotional identification with Mary, standing by the cross and ravaged by grief.

That scene has been presented and appreciated down through the centuries. Like many other soldiers who fought in France and Belgium during the First World War, my own father found himself in a terrain of wayside shrines, representations of Christ on the cross with the Virgin Mary keeping her vigil at the feet of her crucified Son. Often scarred and badly damaged by shells and bullets, those shrines gave soldiers on both sides the feeling of Jesus as their brother and Mary as their mother in the terrible pain and suffering that they faced. Jesus and Mary had drawn close to them in their terrifying situation. My father and other Catholic soldiers remembered what they had sung during the Stations of the Cross: a dramatic, medieval hymn describing the sufferings of the Virgin Mary during her Son's passion and crucifixion called the *Stabat Mater* ("the Mother was standing [at the cross]").

But it is a subsequent scene that has been at least as effective in evoking Mary's role in the passion and death of her Son: the *Pietà*. This is a picture or sculpture of Mary holding the dead body of Christ on her lap or in her arms. Countless Christians and others have seen the *Pietà* by Michelangelo in St. Peter's Basilica, or at least a photograph or replica of it. Created when the artist was in his early twenties, this dramatically intense work represents the Virgin Mary holding the body of her Son across her lap and grieving over his death. Yet the physical beauty of the two bodies takes away something of the grief and suffering from an emotionally charged scene.

Later in his life, Michelangelo carved other versions of the *Pietà*. One is now kept in the museum of the cathedral in Florence. In frustration over what he believed to be a "failure," Michelangelo mutilated and abandoned it, only for the work to be restored and completed by another artist. Its last version is the Rondanini *Pietà* (in the Castello Sforzesco, Milan), on which Michelangelo was still working only a few days before his death when he was almost ninety. The work in Florence places Nicodemus above and Mary Magdalene on the left, helping the Virgin Mary to support the body, which has been taken down from the cross. Her face is close to the face of her dead Son, and she is interlaced with him in a painful union that merges their two bodies physically and spiritually. This physical and spiritual union emerges even more powerfully from the unfinished splendor of the Rondanini *Pietà*, which folds the body of the Virgin into that of the dead Christ. This work expresses the inner, even divine beauty of his suffering, rather than the external beauty of a young "athlete" dying in the prime of life.

Thus far I have recalled how artists, both famous and anonymous, have expressed Mary's association with her Son's suffering and death. But there are the "later" and "earlier" mysteries of Christ that have inspired artists to portray her. The later mysteries take us through Christ's resurrection, the sending of the Holy Spirit, and Mary's assumption into heaven, right to the end of history and the final glory of heaven. For our book, *Catholicism: The Story of Catholic Christianity*, Mario Farrugia and I chose for the jacket illustration a fourteenth-century miniature showing a later mystery: the Holy Spirit descending on Mary and the apostles at Pentecost.[1] The earlier mysteries take us back to the Annunciation, the Nativity, the Presentation in the Temple, and all the other Joyful Mysteries and Luminous Mysteries celebrated in the rosary.

Like innumerable Christians, I feel inspired by images of Mary holding her newborn baby in her arms. To be sure, he does not appear in many wonderful paintings of the Annunciation left us by fifteenth-century Florentines and artists of other times and places. We see only Mary, the angel Gabriel, and sometimes one or two other figures. Christ's conception and birth are being announced; he is not yet visibly there. Nevertheless, he is not absent, as Andy Warhol (1928–87) brilliantly showed in his adaptation of an ancient masterpiece, a painting of the Annunciation by Leonardo da Vinci (1452–1519). Warhol kept only the hands of Mary and the angel; between them he highlighted a mountain that one barely glimpsed in Leonardo's original painting. The change accents effectively the coming down "from above" of the divine Word in Christ's conception and birth. Even in the Annunciation and other compositions where Mary visibly stands or kneels alone, her Son is not missing. He is invisibly present.

What ultimately matters here is that Mary conceived, gave birth to, and mothered the One who was and is personally the Son of God and Savior of the world. When I pray before statues or pictures of Mary holding her divine child, I feel myself understood and cherished by this woman and this mother, and empowered by her Son. During my three years of doctoral studies in England and at the University of Cambridge (1965–68), struggles and panic sometimes drove me to the Church of Our Lady and the English Martyrs, which is blessed by a sixteenth-century statue of the Madonna and Child carved in dark wood. Sometimes it was enough to light a candle, kneel, and pray there in silence. Inevitably, when the thesis was completed and submitted, I went off to express my thanks at the nearby shrine of Our Lady of Walsingham.

In the Middle Ages, the village of Walsingham (in Norfolk) ranked fourth as a place of pilgrimage after Rome, Jerusalem, and Compostela. It was the only one of the four to be dedicated specifically to Our Lady and dates back to the middle of the eleventh century. Each year, thousands of pilgrims once again visit the Shrine of Walsingham, alone or in busloads of groups. In the summer, the fields around Walsingham fill up with tents and caravans, when innumerable young people come to pray and renew their Christian faith. The New Dawn in the Church Conference, a charismatic gathering, currently attracts several thousand people for five days of prayer at the shrine.

Like many priests and other Christians, I have always venerated Mary as the loving helper of the suffering and a compassionate advocate for sinful human beings. Statues of Mary with her Son, stained-glass portrayals from medieval cathedrals, and Eastern icons from all centuries present Marian devotion at its best and truest, with Mary's beauty, nobility, and importance all derived through the Holy Spirit and from her Son.

Prayers, Poetry, and Music

A fourth-century papyrus gives us a Greek version of the first text of *Sub Tuum Presidium,* one of the oldest Christian prayers after those found in the Bible (e.g., the Psalms in the Old Testament, and the Lord's Prayer in the New Testament). It begins: "Beneath your protective shelter we flee, holy Mother of God." This prayer, in an expanded form, continued to be used in the Middle Ages and beyond. Like the rosary with its Joyful, Sorrowful, and Glorious Mysteries—and, since 2002, the Luminous Mysteries—that commemorate the main stages in the story of Christ, the *Sub Tuum Presidium* moves from Mary to her Son: "O glorious and blessed Virgin, our dear Lady, our mediator, our advocate, lead us to your Son, recommend us to your Son, present us to your Son."

Many of these ancient prayers and poems that celebrate the Virgin Mary have been set to music, like one anonymous medieval poem that I have always found very moving: "I sing of a maiden." It honors Mary in a way that suits the Advent and Christmas season. The opening verse: "I sing of a maiden that is makeless [matchless], King of all kinges to her Son she ches [choose]." The poem describes Christ being conceived as silently as the dew falling on the grass in April and ends: "Mother and maiden was never none but she; well may such a lady Goddess mother be." In a courtly and charming manner, this poem honors Mary and does so precisely because of her Son.

Musical composers have ensured much continuity with the happiest aspects of the ancient veneration of Jesus' Mother. Among the oldest Marian antiphons, the Salve Regina ("Hail Holy Queen, Mother of Mercy") dates back at least to the end of the eleventh century. Its tenderly devotional language and its exquisite setting in Gregorian chant have made it enduringly popular in the Catholic world and beyond. Three other ancient Marian antiphons are also much loved: Alma Redemptoris Mater ("Kind Mother of the Redeemer"), Ave Regina Coelorum ("Hail Queen of the Heavens"), and Regina Coeli ("Queen of Heaven").

Living in Rome for over thirty years, I have become even more appreciative of the fifteenth-century Litany of Loreto. Its name comes from the Marian pilgrimage site near the Adriatic coast. It enumerates various titles and qualities of the Virgin Mary (e.g., "Holy Mother of God," "Seat of Wisdom," "Comforter of the Afflicted"), and adds the invocation, "Pray for us." Eventually it was set to music by Mozart.

Along with the Ave Maria (inspired by Lk 1:28, 42–43) and the Magnificat (Lk 1:46–55), the Stabat Mater and the four major Marian antiphons (mentioned above) were set to music by Bach, Brahms, Dvorak, Gounod, Haydn, Palestrina, Schubert, Verdi, Vivaldi, and other famous composers. Not all of them composed settings for every one of these texts, but some of them composed many settings for one or another of the Marian antiphons and prayers. For instance, Palestrina left more than thirty settings for the Magnificat, and Vivaldi came up with four settings for the Salve Regina. The most celebrated setting of all is arguably Bach's composition for the Magnificat. Such music conveys best of all the enduring place of Mary in my life and has provided me with lasting and powerful memories.

At a wedding I celebrated more than twenty years ago in a side chapel of St. Peter's Basilica, an Italian tenor sang, at the beginning of Mass, the "Ave Maria" by Gounod and at the end, Schubert's "Ave Maria." The music brought Mary very powerfully into the married life that the couple was starting. Shortly after September 11, 2001, I watched a program featuring the British soprano Lesley Garrett and dedicated to the people of New York. Garrett conveyed to me a deep sense of Mary's loving concern when she sang from Verdi's *The Force of Destiny*, Leonora's plea to the Virgin to secure her pardon and protection.

Churches

Many priests and other Catholics are ready to name their favorite church or cathedral dedicated to the Blessed Virgin Mary. My first choice is the Basilica of St. Mary Major, where I have often gone to pray. It leaves a deep impression on many visitors to Rome, and not least through the sweep of Catholic history in which it incorporates Marian devotion. In the square outside, the fluted column that carries a seventeenth-century statue of Mary came from a fourth-century public building constructed by Emperor Constantine. Completed in 440, the interior of the church retains its original magnificence with thirty-six marble columns and four granite ones dividing the nave from the aisles, and following the style of a Roman basilica or hall for public administration. Exquisite fifth-century mosaics along the nave and over the triumphal arch depict scenes from the stories of the Old Testament patriarchs, the life of Moses, and the early life of Christ. Down to the nineteenth century, generations have added their statues, pavements, mosaics, chapels, altars, tombs, and the rest—in honor of Jesus and his Mother. One twelfth-century mosaic sets her on the same throne as Christ, and recalls how the Council of Ephesus (431) declared her to be *Theotokos* or Mother of God. What one sees in St. Mary Major evokes many episodes in the history of the Church and the world. For instance, the basilica contains the first figures ever made for a Christmas crèche or crib, those created by Arnolfo di Cambio and his assistants (late thirteenth century). The elaborate ceiling of St. Mary Major, gilded with what is said to be the first gold brought back by Christopher Columbus and presented to the Pope, evokes the love for the Virgin Mary of the Spanish rulers, Ferdinand V of Aragon and Isabella of Castile.

Outside Rome, I have been drawn to other Marian shrines, in particular, to the Gothic cathedral of Chartres. The rich sculpture, stained glass and luminous structure of Chartres Cathedral (southwest of Paris) have always inspired superlatives. A descendant of two American presidents, Henry Adams (1838–1918), wrote, "If you want to know what churches were made for, come down here on some great festival of the Virgin, and give yourself up to it; but come alone! That kind of knowledge cannot be taught and can seldom be shared."[2] Even before reading Adams, I was drawn to Chartres by Charles Peguy (1873–1914). He died heroically at the front in the opening weeks of the First World War. Yet Peguy left a lasting tribute to Mary by helping to promote Chartres Cathedral as a goal of modern pilgrims. Its forty-four window groupings depict a vast array of Old and New Testament scenes and persons, especially of Christ and his Mother.

Mariology

As a member of a teaching order, I have spent most of my years after ordination teaching several fields of theology. As part of my work in Christology,[3] I have been repeatedly drawn to defend and explore the virginal conception of Jesus. So often inaccurately called the virgin birth, the virginal conception involves Mary conceiving Jesus through the power of the Holy Spirit and without the cooperation of a human father. Thus, this belief maintains that Christ's incarnation did not follow the ordinary, inner-worldly laws of procreation, but was the fruit of a special action by the Holy Spirit.

Over many centuries, various difficulties have been raised against the virginal conception. First, there are some who will have no truck with non-natural explanations. Hence, they reject the virginal conception along with the miracles of Jesus, his bodily resurrection, and other such special acts of God. The debate with them goes far beyond the virginal conception and concerns questions of divine causality, special and otherwise. Second, others have argued that pagan stories about male deities impregnating human women to produce extraordinary children prompted Christians to construct the legend of the virginal conception. But the alleged parallels (which regularly involve sexual intercourse and figures who do not belong to history as Mary did) are farfetched. Such legends are quite different from the non-sexual virginal conception reported by Matthew and Luke.[4]

Third, further objections have come from those who argue that these two evangelists did not intend to communicate some historical truth about the miraculous way in which Jesus was conceived, but *merely* aimed to express faith in his unique role and status as Son of God and Messiah. This position normally presupposes (without argument) an alternative: *either* the reports of the virginal conception involve some historical information, *or* they are simply theological reflections. But why not both?

Could not, or rather should not, the reports of the virginal conception embody information *and* some truths of revelation? In Catholic thinking, historical fact and theological reflection repeatedly support and reinforce each other. Catholic theology has been good about not detaching historical and physical reality from theological meaning.

But I strongly suspect that it has been difficulties at the level of meaning that have led people to doubt or reject the fact of the virginal conception. What then might be the religious and saving significance of the virginal conception? The major value of his virginal conception has been to express Jesus' divine sonship. The fact that he was born of a woman pointed to his humanity. The fact that he was born of a virgin pointed to his divinity. But this interpretation should be fitted into the wider pattern of significance: his relationship to the Father in the Spirit. There was a trinitarian face to the whole story of Jesus, from his conception through the creative power of the Holy Spirit.

The virginal conception also has valuable things to say about human salvation. Christ's conception, in initiating the saving drama of the new creation, shows that redemption comes as divine gift. Like the original creation of the world, the new creation is the work of God and pure grace—to be received by human beings, just as Mary received the new life in her womb.

All of what I have written here simply samples how I have experienced in my life as a Catholic and then as a priest the presence of Mary. From my earliest years, I have felt cherished and protected by her. I simply cannot imagine my ministry as a priest without the constant company of Jesus and his beautiful Mother.

Concluding Remarks

Rev. Msgr. Stephen J. Rossetti

The witness of these authors is inspiring. They are exemplary priests, each of whom has a strong, personal Marian devotion. Their witness suggests to me that there are many other priests who also have a passionate devotion to Our Lady. It is clear, then, that many of Mary's priest-sons have not forgotten her.

But for those who have let this important part of their priestly spirituality languish, now is the time to re-energize it. Remember the important graces that come to us through the hands of Mary. She brings us closer to her Son: "Do whatever he tells you." She is the woman clothed with the sun whose heel strikes at the serpent; thus, she is our protector in our fight against evil. The Virgin Mother is a unique grace and strength for us to live out our celibate chastity with integrity. Mary reminds us of the feminine side of God and constantly showers us with this loving, feminine tenderness.

But most importantly, when our road becomes barren and when we ourselves, like Jesus, are nailed to the cross, she will be our faithful companion. When others had left the terrible hill of Golgotha, she did not. Neither will she abandon us. For many priests, the challenges of these last few years, including the Church crisis, have been a tremendous trial. On the cross, Jesus fulfilled his priestly sacrifice of love. In these days we, too, are fulfilling our priesthood in a profound, if sometimes painful way. *We need this woman now more than ever.*

For those priests whose Marian spirituality is very much alive in a personal way, now is the time to give strong, public witness to this dynamic reality. It is time for us to give witness to the importance of the first and perfect disciple of Jesus. A Marian spirituality is more than a private devotion. It is an essential part of our Christian spirituality as given to us directly by Jesus. He is our one Lord and Savior who told us, "Behold your Mother." If we do not publicly include this in our preaching and teaching, we may be depriving others of a wonderful grace. If we do not preach and teach about this woman, can we say we are being completely faithful to the fullness of our Christian life and to the command that Jesus has given us? After being elected Pope, Benedict XVI reiterated the necessity of a Marian spirituality: "We do not praise God sufficiently by keeping silent about his saints, especially Mary, 'the Holy One' who became his dwelling place on earth."[1]

In the midst of the crisis, John Paul II said that a renewal of the Church is "urgently needed."[2] Moreover, this renewal of the Church must go hand in hand with a renewal of the clergy: "In a very real way, the renewal of the Church is linked to the renewal of the priesthood."[3] Mary will lead us to Jesus, he to whom we are configured in our ordination. Thus, she leads us to our authentic selves. One might therefore say that *a renewal of the clergy begins with Mary and ends with Jesus.*

I close with one of the most beautiful lines written by the Fathers of the Second Vatican Council: "Let the entire body of the faithful pour forth persevering prayer to the Mother of God and Mother of Men" (LG 69).

If some part of this book has touched you, I ask you to join in saying the following prayer, dedicating your priestly life to the Mother of Jesus:

A Priest's Act of Dedication to the Blessed Virgin Mary

Most Holy Virgin Mary,
perfect disciple of Jesus,
I come to dedicate my life and my priestly ministry
to your Immaculate Heart.
With Jesus, I desire to abandon myself
to the will of the Father,
and to walk in faith with you, my Mother.
To you I entrust my life in the priesthood.
I give you every gift I possess of nature and of grace,
my body and soul,
all that I own and everything I do.
Pray for me, that the Holy Spirit
may visit me with His many gifts.
Pray with me, that by faith
I may know the power of Christ
and by love make Him present in the world.
Amen.[4]

Contributors

Rev. Louis J. Cameli is pastor of Divine Savior Parish in Chicago and former Director of Ongoing Formation for Priests in the Archdiocese of Chicago. He is the author of *Going to God Together* (Thomas More, 2002) and *Mary's Journey* (Christian Classics, 2003).

Rev. Msgr. Fernando Ferrarese is an Episcopal Vicar in the Diocese of Brooklyn, New York. He has served as pastor at St. Augustine Parish in Park Slope and St. Athanasius Parish in Bensonhurst, and also as Vocation Director for the diocese before beginning his current ministry.

Rev. Anthony J. Figueiredo is an official of the Pontifical Council *Cor Unum*, Vatican City State. He has served in various capacities at Seton Hall University and as assistant to Pope John Paul II at six synods.

Rev. Benedict J. Groeschel, C.F.R., renowned author and spiritual director, is Director of the Office for Spiritual Development of the Archdiocese of New York. He has worked with priests as a retreat leader and spiritual director for more than thirty years.

Rev. Gerald O'Collins, S.J., recently retired as professor of theology at Gregorian University, Rome. He has

published hundreds of articles in popular and professional journals and has authored or co-authored forty-
four books.

Rev. Wilfred (Willy) Raymond, C.S.C., a priest of the
Congregation of Holy Cross and immediate past Pro-
vincial Superior of its Eastern Province, has served as
National Director of Family Theater Productions in Los
Angeles since September 2000.

Rev. Msgr. Walter R. Rossi is a priest of the Diocese of
Scranton who currently serves as Rector of the Basilica
of the National Shrine of the Immaculate Conception in
Washington, D.C.

Most Rev. Arthur J. Serratelli is Bishop of the Diocese
of Paterson, New Jersey. He has taught theology at
numerous seminaries and holds a Licentiate in Sacred
Scripture from the Biblical Institute and a Doctorate in
Sacred Theology from the Gregorian University.

Rev. Msgr. Peter J. Vaghi is pastor of Little Flower Parish
in Bethesda, Maryland. Prior to his seminary studies
at the Gregorian University in Rome, he practiced law.
He remains a member of the Virginia and Washington,
D.C. Bar and is Chaplain to the John Carroll Society. He
has written a number of articles for *America* and *Priest*
magazines.

Rev. Msgr. Stephen J. Rossetti, editor of *Behold Your
Mother*, is the President and CEO of Saint Luke Institute
in Silver Spring, Maryland and Chair of the Board and
CEO of St. Luke's Centre in Manchester, England. He
is a priest of the Diocese of Syracuse and previously
served in two diocesan parishes. He is a licensed

psychologist with a PhD in psychology from Boston College and a Doctor of Ministry from the Catholic University of America. He is the author of scores of articles and several books including *The Joy of Priesthood*—recipient of a Catholic Press Association book award (Ave Maria Press, 2005), and *When the Lion Roars* (Ave Maria Press, 2003). He lectures to priests and religious internationally on priestly spirituality and wellness issues.

Notes

Introduction
Rev. Msgr. Stephen J. Rossetti

1. Hans Urs von Balthasar, "Mary in the Church's Doctrine and Devotion," in *Mary: The Church at the Source,* trans. Adrian Walker (San Francisco: Ignatius Press, 1997), 115.
2. Quotations from the Documents of Vatican II are taken from *The Documents of Vatican II,* ed. Walter M. Abbott, SJ (New York: Herder and Herder, 1966).
3. von Bathasar, 114–115.
4. Joseph Cardinal Ratzinger, "Hail, Full of Grace: Elements of Marian Piety According to the Bible," in *Mary: The Church at the Source,* 62.
5. Ibid., 63.
6. John Paul II, *Redemptoris Mater,* (March 25, 1987), no. 6, www.vatican.va.

Chapter 1: At the School of the Mother: The Marian Spirituality of John Paul II
Rev. Anthony J. Figueiredo

1. Abbé Francis Trochu, *The Curé d'Ars: St. Jean-Marie Baptiste Vianney* (Westminister, MD: Newman Press, 1950), 10.

2. John Paul II, *Gift and Mystery: On the Fiftieth Anniversary of My Priestly Ordination* (New York: Doubleday, 1996), 20.
3. Jerzy Peterkiewicz, trans., *Collected Poems: Karol Wojtyla* (New York: Random House, 1979), 2.
4. Ibid., 50.
5. Pope John Paul II, General Audience (June 30, 1993), www .vatican.va.
6. Ibid.
7. John Paul II, Holy Thursday Letter, *Behold, Your Mother*, no. 4., www.vatican.va.
8. John Paul II, *Gift and Mystery*, 27–31.
9. John Paul II, Homily at Fatima (May 13, 1982), www.vatican .va.
10. St. John Marie Vianney, *Catechism on the Blessed Virgin*.
11. John Paul II, *Gift and Mystery*, 20.
12. George Weigel, *Witness to Hope: The Biography of Pope John Paul II* (New York: HarperCollins, 1999), 68.
13. *Insegnamenti di Giovanni Paolo II*, 2 (1982): 2442–43.
14. John Paul II, *Memory and Identity: Personal Reflections* (New York: Rizzoli, 2005), 190.
15. John Paul II, Address to Mariological Colloquium, *L'Osservatore Romano*, English edition (October 25, 2000).
16. André Frossard, *Be Not Afraid! John Paul II Speaks Out on His Life, His Beliefs and His Inspiring Vision for Humanity* (New York: St. Martin's Press, 1984), 125.
17. *True Devotion to the Blessed Virgin*, no. 233. This work can be found in *God Alone: The Collected Writings of St. Louis Marie de Montfort* (Bay Shore, NY: Montfort Publications, 1988).
18. *Rule of the Missionary Priests of the Company of Mary*, no. 62, www .ewtn.com/library/Montfort/RULECOM.HTM.
19. *True Devotion*, no. 62.
20. *True Devotion*, nos. 55–58.

Chapter 2: Mother of Every Priestly Grace
Rev. Msgr. Fernando Ferrarese

1. Dante Alighieri, *Paradiso*, in The Divine Comedy, trans. Rev. Philip H. Wicksteed (London: J.M. Dent & Co., 1903), 393.
2. Gerard Manley Hopkins, *Poems and Prose of Gerard Manley Hopkins*, ed. W. H. Gardner (Baltimore, MD: Penguin Books, 1953), 56.
3. Georges Bernanos, *Diary of a Country Priest* (New York: Carroll & Graf Publishers, Inc., 1987), 211.

Chapter 3: Mary, the Pope and the American Apostle of the Family Rosary
Rev. Willy Raymond, C.S.C.

1. Henry Adams, *Mont-Saint Michel and Chartres* (New York: The New American Library of Literature, 1961), 105.
2. Walter J. Burghardt, S.J., *Long Have I Loved You: A Theologian Reflects on His Church* (Maryknoll, NY: Orbis Books, 2000), 308.
3. Scott Hahn, *Hail, Holy Queen* (New York: Doubleday, 2001), 140.
4. Loretta Young, *The Joyful Mysteries*, (Hollywood, CA: Family Theater Productions, 1985), introductory comments by Miss Young on camera.
5. Patrick Peyton, C.S.C., *The Story of Father Patrick Peyton, C.S.C. and The Family Rosary* (Albany, NY: The Family Rosary Inc., 1996), 1–7. Used by permission.
6. Patrick Peyton, C.S.C., *Father Peyton's Rosary Prayer Book* (San Francisco: Ignatius Press, 2003), 287.
7. Benedict XVI, *Deus Caritas Est* (December 24, 2005), www.vatican.va.

Chapter 4: Mary, Mother of God and Mother of the Church, Walks with Her Son's Priests
Rev. Louis J. Cameli

1. I have explored this point in: Louis J. Cameli, *Going to God Together* (Allen, TX: Thomas More, 2002).
2. See *Redemptoris Mater,* especially Part II: "The Mother of God at the Center of the Pilgrim Church."
3. I have studied this dimension of priestly ministry and spirituality in greater detail in: Louis J. Cameli, *Ministerial Consciousness: A Biblical-Spiritual Study* (in *Analecta Gregoriana,* 198) (Rome: Universita Gregoriana Editrice, 1975).
4. Gerard Manley Hopkins, *Poems and Prose of Gerard Manley Hopkins,* ed. W. H. Gardner (Baltimore, MD: Penguin Books, 1953), 55.

Chapter 5: Priests' Response in the Face of Reports of Marian Private Revelations
Rev. Benedict J. Groeschel, C.F.R.

1. Benedict J. Groeschel, C.F.R., *A Still, Small Voice* (San Francisco: Ignatius Press, 1993).
2. Any good theological library will have a copy of Fr. Poulain's work, originally published as *Des Grâces d'Oraison* in 1901 and in English translation in 1910. After being out of print for many years, it was reissued in a facsimile edition (London: R. A. Kessinger, 1997). See also Augustin Poulain, S.J., *Revelations and Visions* (Staten Island, NY: Alba House, 1998), which is a reprint of Part IV of the larger work.
3. Lincoln Barnett, *The Universe and Dr. Einstein,* with a Foreword by Albert Einstein (New York: William Morrow and Company, 1968), 105–106.
4. Sandra L. Zimdars-Swartz, *Encountering Mary* (Princeton, NJ: Princeton University Press, 1991). See also Ruth Harris, *Lourdes: Body and Spirit in the Secular Age* (New York: Penguin Press, 1999).

5. An example further back in history is the appearance of the Blessed Virgin at Guadalupe.
6. See Alexis Carrel, *The Voyage to Lourdes* (Port Huron, MI: Real-View Books, 1994). See also Benedict J. Groeschel, C.F.R., *Why Do We Believe?* (Huntington, IN: Our Sunday Visitor, 2005), 72–76 for a brief account of Dr. Carrel's experience at Lourdes.
7. Barnett, 105.

Chapter 6: Mary: The Perspective of a Parish Priest
Rev. Msgr. Peter J. Vaghi

1. John Paul II, *Rosarium Virginis Mariae*, (October 23, 2004), 1, www.vatican.va.
2. Paul VI, *Marialis Cultus* (February 2, 1974), 42, www.vatican.va.
3. Benedict XVI, "Eucharistic Concelebration with the New Cardinals," (March 25, 2006), www.vatican.va.

Chapter 7: Mary's House
Rev. Msgr. Walter R. Rossi

1. Benedict XVI, "Encounter with Men and Women Religious, Seminarians and Representatives of Ecclesial Movements" (May 26, 2006), www.vatican.va.
2. John Paul II, "Address to the Bishops of Michigan and Ohio Making Their *Ad Limina* Visit" (May 21, 1998), www.vatican.va.
3. John Paul II, "Priests Must Foster Devotion to Mary" (June 30, 1993), www.vatican.va. See also *Catechism of the Catholic Church*, 2d ed. (Citta del Vaticano: Libreria Editrice Vaticana, 1997 / Washington, D.C.: United States Catholic Conference, 1997), nos. 2673–79.
4. *Behold Your Mother: Woman of Faith, A Pastoral Letter on the Blessed Virgin Mary*, National Conference of Catholic Bishops (Washington, D.C.: United States Catholic Conference, 1973), 45.
5. See Benedict XVI, *Deus Caritas Est*, no. 41.
6. Richard Cardinal Cushing, *Mary* (Boston: St. Paul Editions, 1963), 49.

7. Josemaria Escriva, *The Way* (New York: Sceptor Publishers, 1982), 166.
8. *Catechism of the Catholic Church*, no. 495 and no. 963.
9. Benedict XVI, "Homily on the Solemnity of the Assumption of the Blessed Virgin Mary" (August 15, 2005), www.vatican.va.
10. John XXIII, *Journal of a Soul*, trans. Dorothy White (New York: McGraw-Hill Book Company, 1965), 359.
11. John Paul II, *Rosarium Virginis Mariae*, nos. 3 and 26.

Chapter 8: Mary and the Divine Presence: A Biblical Reflection
Most Rev. Arthur J. Serratelli

1. Raymond E. Brown et al., *Mary in the New Testament* (Philadelphia: Fortress Press, 1978), 52–55.
2. Raymond E. Brown, *The Birth of the Messiah* (New York: Doubleday, 1977), 316–319.
3. Jean Galot, *Mary in the Gospel* (Maryland: The Newman Press, 1965), 2.
4. John McHugh, *The Mother of Jesus in the New Testament* (New York: Doubleday, 1975), 60–62.
5. Galot, 22–25.
6. Lucien Deiss, *Mary, Daughter of Sion*, trans. Barbara T. Blair (Collegeville, MN: The Liturgical Press, 1972), 76–79; McHugh, 56–63.
7. Andre Feuillet, *Jesus and His Mother* (Petersham, MA: St. Bede's Publication, 1977), 110–112.
8. Pope John Paul II, "Annual Address to the Roman Curia," in *L'Osservatore Romano*, English edition (January 11, 1988), 6–8.

Chapter 9: She Will Crush His Head
Rev. Msgr. Stephen J. Rossetti

1. Pius IX, *Ineffabilis Deus*, 17, DS 2803.
2. Gabriele Amorth, *An Exorcist Tells His Story*, trans. Nicolette V.

MacKenzie (San Francisco: Ignatius Press, 1999), 49.

3. Thomas Merton, *Prayer: The Search for Inner Rest*, audio-cassette (Kansas City, MO: Credence Communications,), n.d.

4. Trochu, 251–252.

5. Von Balthasar, 117.

Chapter 10: Mary, Catholicism, and Priesthood
Rev. Gerald O'Collins, S.J.

1. Gerald O'Collins, S.J., and Mario Farrugia, *Catholicism. The Story of Catholic Christianity* (New York: Oxford University Press, 2003).

2. Adams, 117.

3. See Gerald O'Collins, *Interpreting Jesus* (Ramsey, NJ: Paulist Press, 1983), 195–200; *Christology* (New York: Oxford University Press, 1995), 273–78; *Incarnation* (New York: Continuum, 2002), 99–111.

4. Brown, 522–24, 602–03.

Concluding Remarks
Rev. Msgr. Stephen J. Rossetti

1. Benedict XVI, "Homily on the Solemnity of the Assumption."

2. John Paul II, "To the Cardinals of the United States" (April 23, 2002), www.vatican.va.

3. John Paul II, "To the Bishops of the Ecclesiastical Provinces of Boston and Hartford (U.S.A.) on Their *Ad Limina* Visit" (September 2, 2004), citing *Optatam Totius*, no. 1.

4. Copyright St. Vincent's Ministry to Priests, P. O. Box 1559, Palm Harbor, Florida 34682, U.S.A. (tel: 727-784-6462). Used by permission.

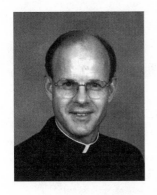

A priest of the Diocese of Syracuse and a licensed psychologist, Monsignor Stephen J. Rossetti spent six years as an intelligence officer after graduating from the Air Force Academy in 1973. He holds a PhD in psychology from Boston College and a Doctor of Ministry degree from The Catholic University of America. He previously served in two parishes and is currently President and CEO of Saint Luke Institute, a treatment program for clergy and religious in Silver Spring, Maryland.

Msgr. Rossetti is recipient of a Proclaim Award by the USCCB, a Distinguished Priest Award from the John Carroll Society of the Archdiocese of Washington, D.C., and an Alumnus Lifetime Service Award from the Theological College of Catholic University.

Msgr. Rossetti lectures internationally, presenting workshops on clergy and religious spirituality, mental health, and wellness. He is the author of *When the Lion Roars* and *The Joy of Priesthood* (both from Ave Maria Press).

More Favorites from **Stephen J. Rossetti**

The Joy of Priesthood

Invites priests to recognize the dignity of their calling through honest and psychologically based self-assessment—because happiness in the priesthood flows from both wholeness and holiness. Fr. Rosetti also emphasizes the need for accountability, honesty on all levels, stronger relationships between bishops and priests, and changes in seminary formation.

ISBN: 9781594710667 / 224 pages / $15.95

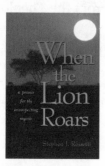

When the Lion Roars
A Primer for the Unsuspecting Mystic

Becoming a mystic is not a matter of learning some "mystical secret," but of entering into the divine simplicity of God's unbounded and unrestrained love. Addresses questions and concerns that arise on the path to deeper prayer. Draws from the wisdom of scripture and guides us on a road we may never have expected to take.

ISBN: 9780877939856 / 160 pages / $11.95

ave maria press®

Available from your bookstore or from
ave maria press / Notre Dame, IN 46556
www.avemariapress.com / Ph: 800-282-1865
A Ministry of the Indiana Province of Holy Cross

Keycode: FØAØ8Ø7ØØØØ